2018

Wr...
...
Disorders program at
WCU.

Mean Christianity

Mean Christianity

Finding Our Way Back to Christ's Likeness

BILLY T. OGLETREE

RESOURCE *Publications* · Eugene, Oregon

MEAN CHRISTIANITY
Finding Our Way Back to Christ's Likeness

Resource Publications
An Imprint of Wipf and Stock Publishers
199 W. 8th Ave., Suite 3
Eugene, OR 97401

www.wipfandstock.com

PAPERBACK ISBN: 978-1-5326-4606-5
HARDCOVER ISBN: 978-1-5326-4607-2
EBOOK ISBN: 978-1-5326-4608-9

Manufactured in the U.S.A.   03/01/18

To my loving parents, Powell and Frances Ogletree—two "all-in" Christians and wonderful life models. Thank you for always "playing your position" with me and others.

Contents

Acknowledgments

Julie, thank you for your undying belief in this project, not to mention your enthusiasm and assistance throughout. In every way, you complete me. Erica, Frances Bess, Sabrina, and Mittie, thank you for your amazing editorial guidance. Finally, thanks to the many others who read early manuscript drafts or helped in countless other ways to make this book a reality.

Introduction

This book is not something that emerged from years of thought or planning. In fact, I got the idea during the Christmas holiday of 2016. For several years, however, I have felt God's guidance in the area of faith-based writing, and I found a publication outlet, an online devotional series, for which I've written for two years. The idea of a book never crossed my mind until a few short months ago.

There are times in life when one's purpose is clear. Maybe an everyday task becomes your obsession, or an epiphany overwhelmingly drives you. That is the way I feel about this book. I believe what follows must be said—in fact, I think we, as members of the body of Christ, are at a historical crossroads. We can choose to continue to drift away from Christ's call to inclusiveness and love, or we can embrace these principles in a life-altering, world-changing way.

My intent is to explore Christianity as an intentional, daily commitment to others—a cathartic and uncomfortable journey that leads travelers to Christ's likeness. I will consider how and why individual Christians and the corporate body of Christ have come to be perceived negatively by so many. Let's face it: one of the reasons you picked up this book is its title, *Mean Christianity*. This notion resonates with the experiences of countless individuals, yet it is absolutely antithetical to Christ and His teaching.

It is my hope that you approach the pages that follow with an open mind. As you will read, I don't have unusual insights or special theological training. I am just a sinner redeemed by God's love, forgiveness, and grace. This said, I truly believe that what I offer is not mine to give, but His to share.

Billy T. Ogletree
December 2017

CHAPTER I

Who Am I?
Why This Book?
Why Now?

I entered this project headlong, with a great sense of calling and commitment. Two months and two chapters later, I started to think about publication. As a professor, I was familiar with the typical academic publication process. This, however, was no typical project for me. I was wading in unfamiliar waters.

I took a risk and contacted Barbara Brown Taylor, an accomplished American Episcopal priest, professor, author, and theologian. To my great surprise, she responded with encouragement and one daunting comment. Professor Taylor shared that publishers of faith-based nonfiction typically seek authors with strong, recognizable platforms—authors who offer their work with some degree of authority because of who they are and whom they can reach.

While I have such a platform as a professor, a speech-language pathologist who has spent a lifetime serving and writing about individuals with severe disabilities and autism, this book addresses a different topic altogether. I was going out on a thin limb.

For the next several months I considered my platform as a Christian author. I came to the conclusion that it's a work in progress. The foundation of my platform was laid with a decision to follow Jesus as a child and my subsequent fifty-plus-year Christian journey. This foundation was built upon with an intense love of writing, an interest in a deeper relationship with God at age fifty, and a clear call to faith-based writing about four years ago. To be honest, I think God's been working on me, readying me for this and possibly future projects. All I know for certain is that He wanted me to share the message you are about to read.

This book is written for Christians. That said, I welcome curious readers of other faiths or no faith, or, for that matter, anyone who has encountered Christian meanness. To provide clarity and context for my calling and this book, I begin by answering three questions: Who am I? Why this book? Why now?

WHO AM I?

So, who am I? I am a sixty-year-old who lives in the beautiful mountains of western North Carolina. I was born in south Mississippi, the third child of two loving Christian parents. I enjoyed a charmed childhood in a lovely, moderate-size university town. My formative life experiences revolved around church activities in a vibrant faith community.

I vividly remember attending a revival service as a third-grader (my teacher invited me to her church), where I accepted Christ and began a lifelong journey as a Christian. My childhood was quite sheltered. Although the civil rights movement and the Vietnam War were predominant issues of the day, I don't remember encountering them other than through brief news stories that seemed unrelated to my daily existence.

I lived the life of Opie Taylor (from the *The Andy Griffith Show*). I was, largely unknowingly, a privileged white male in a divided and struggling nation. Early on, I lived in a segregated society. My schools were white, my church was white, my neighbors were white. In fact, my only real contact with people of color was with service staff in various community institutions. Although my world was segregated, the repeated message in my home was one of love and inclusion. My parents never spoke disparagingly of anyone, and it was clear that this was their expectation of me.

A 1971 desegregation order changed my world. For the first time, I had everyday relationships with children of color. This was challenging only because it was unfamiliar. Fear, an emotion I will consider later in this book, created apprehension that quickly evolved to acceptance and friendship. In fact, when I visit my hometown today, I often encounter friends from the ninth grade that I would not have made without mandated deseg-regation. I'm very grateful it occurred.

I mention desegregation because it brought about the first real broad-ening of my world. I came into daily contact with children who had not shared my life experiences—children, black and white, who had not known the advantages of monetary sufficiency or a strong family life. And, largely to my surprise, I also met children of color who were very much like me, who shared many of my life experiences. This began a lifelong lesson I have continued to learn— stereotypic assumptions are anything but reliable.

My high-school years were uneventful to say the least. Life continued to revolve around family, the church, and a very close set of male friends with whom I have largely maintained contact to this day. There were brief brushes with reality outside this small bubble. For example, I recall the in-justice of a segregated senior prom. Though at the time I recognized this as grossly inconsistent with my integrated educational experience, I was not moved to action. I basically lived a passive and risk-free teen life.

It was during my high-school years that I believe I began a very com-mon and societally safe expression of faith. That is, I went to church at least three times weekly, yet I made no real or sustained effort to engage God personally. I maintained this pattern for years, while episodically ex-periencing spiritual highs and lows. My bet is that my experience does not differ from that of most Christians reading this book.

College and graduate school offered several mostly positive, life-broadening influences. Most of my college years I stayed at home (my siblings had moved out) and grew to know and appreciate my parents. I saw firsthand two people with living faiths, individuals who modeled the type of Christianity I now seek to live. My father constantly visited for the church and selflessly gave his time and money. My mother, a wonderful teacher, took special interest in every child she taught, and by doing so, optimized their learning potential. I observed my parents daily and, as I began to mature and become less egocentric, their actions laid down strong guidelines for my life.

College also gave me a vocational life passion. During my freshman year, while working at a local store, I was approached by a well-dressed man who could not speak. He stood two feet away, holding a coat hanger and motioning that his keys were locked in his car. This brief meeting af-fected me profoundly. I had taken successful communication for granted. I dedicated the next five years of my life to becoming a speech-language pathologist. I came to know countless people who struggled with communication—children and adults who could not express themselves intelligibly through speech. I met and worked with friends and family members who hurt as much as their loved ones who were struggling to communicate. I also enjoyed the mentorship of intelligent and diverse professors and preceptors who taught me how to both promote communicative success and see things through the eyes of individuals who were marginalized by their impairments. My initial graduate training occurred five hours from my home, taking me away from my parents and the community of my childhood. For the first time, I encountered peers from other regions of the country whose religious and life experiences were radically different from mine. And yet I learned that they were like me in many ways.

I began to see the world through the eyes of others—to recognize and appreciate difference, whether it related to disability, religion, or life experience. My narrow view of the world, fostered in the controlled environments of south Mississippi, was changing.

Throughout this time, I refined a compartmentalized orientation to life. There was work, there was leisure, and, when there was time (maybe every other Sunday) there was church. (I purposefully say "church" here rather than "faith.") I was comfortable exercising my Christianity in an accepted and easily managed way—on some Sunday mornings.

After graduation, I took my first job to be near a woman I was dating. The position was in a day developmental center for children with intellectual disabilities (ID). Two weeks later my girlfriend ended our relationship, and within another week, I realized that I had found my calling—working with people with ID. Going to work was an incredible joy. Funny how those things happen—I've always viewed my first "real job" through providential lenses.

After a second job in a residential facility for individuals with ID, I returned to school for my doctorate. Four additional years of study brought more experiences with diversity. I learned alongside, as well as was taught by, people very different from me. Many had different religious backgrounds or no active faith. Others were gay or lesbian. Most people I encountered were from different parts of the United States. Again, I found that I shared many core values with my new friends. They were loving and cared deeply for me, as the following story illustrates.

During my studies I lived in a duplex with a fellow doctoral student from Iraq. Ghazi was a large man, an accomplished weight lifter. He and I often shared meals and talked about our faiths. A devout Muslim, Ghazi articulated many positive comparisons between his faith and mine. Late one night, a young man came to my door saying he needed help. I offered to drive him to get some gas for his car. After leaving the duplex, the man became belligerent to the point of violence. As I stopped my vehicle to ask him to get out, Ghazi appeared out of nowhere, exiting his car and coming to my aid. Needless to say, the young man fled quickly.

After earning my doctorate, I started working in a large Midwestern medical center, where I provided clinical services and did some limited teaching. Again, new work and living environments brought me face-to-face with difference. I learned that Midwesterners were delightful. And for the first time, I had to seek out a church to attend since my denomination was in the minority.

The two greatest events of my life at this time were marriage and parenthood. I met my soulmate and the love of my life during my doctoral studies. She has changed me only for the better. Her deep and abiding love for the marginalized and God's creation reinforced my evolving orientation toward inclusiveness. Mind you, this is a woman who will catch a bug and escort it from our house rather than kill it. As a native Mississippian, this was a foreign concept to me. Three years after we married, we became the proud parents of a wonderful daughter, now in divinity school.

My wife, daughter, and I moved to North Carolina in 1992. There I began my now twenty-six-year career as a college professor. Within four years, our family expanded to include our son, now working in the forestry industry. He is a vibrant young man who lives life fully, much more so than I did at his age. Being a father both broadened and narrowed my life. Things expanded as I saw glimpses of the world through small eyes. I saw my children's wonder and their fears, although in hindsight I did this too little. I had yet to emerge into a more intentional day-to-day existence. Things narrowed for me as I became more aware of my role as a provider. In sum, I worried a lot—most often about things over which I had little control.

My professional career progressed nicely as I easily found my place as a university professor. Over the years, I have taught hundreds if not thousands of students, many of whom have gone on to become accomplished therapists and university faculty members. I've enjoyed success as a writer, publishing regularly and assuming regional and national roles in my area of interest: the communication needs of people with severe intellectual disabilities, including autism. I frequently tell those who ask about my job that being a professor is the best job on earth—you get spring break for life.

For our first fifteen or so years in western North Carolina, I continued my compartmentalized approach to life and faith. I have to say, however, that the "church" compartment got pretty big. My young family was at church a lot. In fact, in many ways church was our primary community. My wife and I worked in the nursery, then in the children and youth ministries. We found ourselves engaged in most church events and activities. Generally, we were happy with our involvement. Almost always we were exhausted by it.

Then things began to change for me. I trace this back to my reluctant commitment to spend a week as a chaperone for our church youth group at a retreat at a nearby university. My compartmentalized life stopped. For a week, I encountered God front and center. Whether in dynamic worship services, instructional groups, or during devotional times, I was engaged by my Creator. This was amazing. Upon my return, I'd like to say that nothing was the same, but that would be an exaggeration. But I did begin a very intentional effort to engage God daily. This has taken the form of entering into a sacred space each morning in which He and I talk—where He hears me and increasingly I listen to Him (those who know me know this is a challenge). My prayer life has become something I can't do without. Ever so gradually, I find myself inching closer to an intentional, God-centered existence. Do I fail? Miserably! When it happens, I just try to get up and move forward. Only God's grace allows me to keep walking with Him each day.

I hope you see that my life has not been so special. I openly admit that I've been privileged in terms of life models, resources, and opportunities. I have also grown in positive ways through my encounters with difference. Most importantly, I've had some life-altering epiphanies specific to the role of faith in my life. In sum, faith is not a side show or something to compartmentalize—it *is* the show.

WHY THIS BOOK?

As I wrote in the introduction, I didn't see this book coming. I've felt God's urging to write, but I thought I had it covered with my involvement in a regular devotional series. Then the book title literally popped into my head. I was driving with my family to see my aging mother over the Christmas holidays, and it struck me—*Mean Christianity*. I could see the words! I don't doubt that it surfaced in part due to months of angry rhetoric surrounding the presidential election of 2016. For decades the American people have endured extreme voices on both sides of the political aisle, but in this election season, meanness rose to new levels.

I heard people who espoused Christianity saying things that were inconsistent with Christ and His teaching—things that were exclusionary, painful, and mean. I heard casual conversations in which people expressed their frustration with, even aversion to, Christians. Maybe that created the fertile ground for God to plant the seeds of this book. Simply stated, meanness is not consistent with my Christian experience. I think it is fair to say meanness has no place in anyone's Christian experience. In the pages that follow, I'll try to describe a path back to what I consider the cornerstone of the faith—Christ's likeness.

You have now read my abbreviated life story. What I haven't shared is that I've developed a mantra of sorts to express how I feel Christianity should unfold in one's life. My family and friends have heard it more than once—*play your position*. I'm an avid sports fan, and though baseball is not my favorite sport, my mantra comes from a comparison of baseball and the Christian life.

First, baseball is both an individual and group sport. Individual players make plays alone and with other players. Likewise, in Christianity, we function both individually as Christians and corporately as members of the body of Christ. Second, baseball is both offensive and defensive. The same can be said for Christianity. I am thankful that many people went "on the offensive" to share Christ with me as a child through their words and actions. This said, the most effective Christians in my life, to use baseball vernacular, waited on the right pitch. Their "good eye" offered a message at a welcome time and only after a relationship was formed. It is also worth noting that offense in baseball can be a rarity. I've been to many games in which defense ruled and runs were infrequent. So I believe it is with individual Christianity—you are in the field more than you are at the plate. Third, when playing defense in baseball, you are on your own. A particular area of play is your responsibility. The same can be said for the individual Christian, hence my mantra "play your position." I believe this to simply mean be Christ to the person in front of you. Do it all day, every day. Sure, there will be times when you turn a double play with someone. Maybe you will work with others to meet a particular need that can't be met with your efforts alone. But the everyday in-the-trenches life of a Christian occurs one relationship at a time. Of course, as a Christian you are not alone. You have Christ's presence and the encouragement of a broader body of believers. As a kid in the field that prayed the ball would not be hit to me, I'm thankful I'm not alone.

There is one more piece to this analogy. Who calls the game? I believe God is behind the plate. Read this carefully: God makes the call on the actions (right or wrong in your eyes) of others, their faiths or lack thereof, their lifestyles. I know we all want behind that plate. We so want to adjudicate the injustices in this world. We are absolutely sure we know what is wrong and right—we got this, God! "Oh, just let me call them out, Lord. Don't worry about that log in my eye, I see well enough to spot the twig in theirs."

I'm happy that judgment, at any level and for anything, is not my call. Believe me, it is not yours either. As Christians we are at the very least pretentious, if not irreverent, when we think we share God's mind—His perspective—and when we believe our views and biases are always in one-to-one agreement with God's.

I'm busy enough in this life just playing my position. Judgment is beyond my pay grade. I say this, yet I do judge. This brings me back to the reality that I fail every day. I have to face the fact that, from a baseball perspective, I've made so many errors, I fear being traded. But, I've got that grace thing working for me, so my score card is clean.

We'll revisit this analogy throughout the book. Now it is time to consider my final question.

WHY NOW?

As I mentioned earlier, I'm sixty. I once disregarded aging entirely. My only thought about having a birthday was the knowledge that I would get a card from my father with cash—one dollar for every year lived. My sister, who enjoyed the same annual gift, said it was the only day she wished she was 100! As I hit my forties, age began to matter. Maybe I saw myself slipping past a physical prime, and I became more acutely aware of my mortality. I lost a friend and my father about that time, which jolted me into the reality that my life was finite. Lately, though, I've taken a different approach. Aging hasn't bothered me. In fact, aside from a few more aches and pains and an earlier bedtime, I haven't given it much thought.

With age, I've gotten a little freer with my thoughts, opinions, and actions. This can be good and bad. I care a little less what others think about me, which has led to longer hair, an occasional beard, more casual clothes, and yes, more openness about my faith. Working at a university, you quickly learn that everyone does not see things as you do, that sharing your faith is somewhat taboo, especially with those whom you teach. This said, in recent years I've shared with colleagues and students that I pray for them. I've also offered advice, when approached, from my perspective as a Christian. I mention all of this because I think the right time has come for me to write this book. I have some life under my belt and a few things to share. More importantly, offering my thoughts openly is less challenging now. So, I guess I was ready to write, and God knew this.

The current geopolitical environment is right too. Our world, and more specifically our nation, is incredibly polarized. The country seems split down the middle politically, and the two sides have no interest in affiliation, much less collaboration. In fact, political parties find joy in the opposing side's failures and absolute despair in their successes. I used to be bothered when I would occasionally hear snippets of talk-radio shows that espoused opinions opposed to my own. I learned to let this go by realizing that people simply have different worldviews. This is the only way I could imagine how two individuals or, for that matter, two groups of people, could look at one set of observations or facts and come up with two incompatible interpretations.

But this is not a political book. This is a book about Christianity. While I can acknowledge and accept differing worldviews in the political arena, they should not exist in the expression of the Christian faith. Christians should have a common core that makes them see the world in a similar way. I argue that this common core is Christ—His words and His life. I further argue that our Christian view should be one that is loving, caring, and inclusive.

Will there be differences of opinion in the understanding of Christianity? Absolutely! Some will hold one tenet of the faith dearly while others will emphasize another. As a body of Christ, we may even have differing priorities with respect to serving others. But these differences don't alter my bottom line: Christians need to be Christlike. There is no room for beliefs, attitudes, or actions that fail this litmus test.

I believe the time is right for this book, or more broadly, for an open presentation of Christianity as an expression of Christ's likeness. I've heard it said that Christianity, or for that matter any religion, is one lifetime from extinction, that each successive generation has a responsibility to share the faith with the one that follows. My call is for Christians to be on the same page with what we share. Differences, especially those that appear "mean" and exclusive, make our message hypocritical as well as unattractive.

The world is hurting. It needs a voice of kindness and love. Jesus Christ provides that voice. It is our responsibility as Christians to make sure it is heard as He intended it. Long before Jesus, the prophet Micah summed up a simple but challenging charge for those choosing to follow God: "And what does the Lord require of you, but to do justice, and to love kindness, and to walk humbly with your God" (Mic 6:8). Let's answer that charge daily using the words and actions of Jesus. Just play your position.

CHAPTER 2

What Is Christianity?

Why define Christianity? To speak of mean Christianity, a comparative point of reference is necessary. That is, Christians must understand their faith or what they claim. This chapter is my effort to explore and define Christianity in an attempt to provide context for ideas that follow.

Remember, I am not a theologian. I can only share what Christianity is to me. My beliefs have their origin in the faith of my youth, but they have also been informed by life experiences and, most recently, my efforts at a more intentional walk with Christ. My thoughts about Christianity center on what I will refer to as the primacy of Christ. Simply stated, Christ's coming, life, death, and resurrection, considered collectively, is *the* story of the Bible. His words and His actions, as presented in the canonical gospels (Matthew, Mark, Luke, and John), are what should primarily inform our lives. Why Christ, you ask? As a Christian, I believe that Christ is God incarnate—God in flesh. As God, then, Christ is *the* authority when it comes to my life.

I know many reading this book will ask, "What about books of the Bible other than the gospel texts—those that preceded Christ's life and those, written by His followers, that emerged post resurrection?" They are important. They were God-inspired, and they, too, inform our walk. In fact, you'll find them cited throughout this book. Stories of the Old Testament have tremendous relevance to modern life. History repeats itself, and we need all the help we can get. The New Testament books and letters also address real issues in the early church that are still with us today. Again, there is no denying their value.

My caution with Bible stories, books, and letters that don't specifically share Christ's words and actions is that they can be "cherry-picked." The origin of that term comes from the picker who picks only fruit that is easy to reach. Someone who "cherry-picks" in an argument, then, selectively chooses facts or opinions that support their thoughts or positions. Remember my baseball analogy? I said we all want behind the plate. When cherry-picking the prohibitions of the Bible, the umpires among us are literally in holy heaven. They have all the ammunition needed to judge others. They can "pick" from the more universal sins of pride, lust, or envy, or they can go right to behaviors they find most uncomfortable or aberrant—homosexuality, for example.

Remember who is behind the plate? It isn't you, and it isn't me. God is back there. My God is big enough to make the calls—He doesn't need my help. I just need to play my position. I'm not saying you can't hold personal beliefs about "right" and "wrong" that are informed by God's word. What I mean is this: hold *them*, but don't weaponize them to demonize and ostracize others. I share more about this in Chapter 3.

I've referred to Christianity in both individual and corporate terms. Let's define it based on my idea of Christ's primacy. In my eyes, Christianity is the individual and corporate pursuit of Christ's likeness. It is the minute-to-minute, hour-to-hour, day-to-day emulation of Christ. To emulate is to imitate. So, emulating Christ is imitating Christ. We have all seen "What would Jesus do? (WWJD)" bracelets and bumper stickers. Being a Christian is a commitment to actually live that way—with everyone, including people who disagree with you, who don't look or act like you, who even harbor ill will against you.

As a reader you might say that I've set the bar too high, that you can conceptually agree with me but it is impossible to live that way. My answer is that the Christian life is a journey. The Apostle Paul characterizes it just this way: Christians should be progressing to Christ's likeness. There will be setbacks, but, thank God, there is also grace.

The remainder of this chapter is my exploration of Christ's likeness. I know seminal texts could have guided my efforts. After all, I'm not the first person to examine the life of Jesus. If, however, I solely pursued others' opinions, I could potentially lose my own. Therefore, what follows is my critical review of Jesus' words and actions. I have read and re-read the gospels of Matthew, Mark, Luke, and John. Again, I selected these Bible books because of their emphasis on Jesus' life—their pivotal nature as source material for Jesus' ministry. As you read what follows, remember I'm basing my definition of Christianity on the primacy of Christ.

As a professor, part of my job is to conduct research. For this chapter, I applied a qualitative methodology as I considered the words and actions of Jesus. Qualitative methods allow researchers to examine data sets to identify commonalities and themes. It is my belief that the themes emerging from my research illuminate the basic qualities of Christ's likeness. With these qualities in hand, we can emulate (or imitate) Christ as we work each day to "play our position."

THEMES FROM THE LIFE OF JESUS

Let's make two things clear. First, I know there may be non-Christian readers thinking that Jesus' words were not recorded verbatim and could have been compromised by human interpretation. While this criticism is fair, the presence of corroborating witnesses (the collective writings of the gospels) and the strong tradition of oral history support the validity of gospel texts. To elaborate, we all have enjoyed books, movies, or television mysteries in which corroborating witnesses seal a verdict. When considering the four gospels, there is consistency, if not one-to-one message correspondence. Furthermore, in Christ's day, oral stories persisted with little variance for generations. In the case of stories sharing the words and actions of Jesus, it was a relatively short time between Jesus' death and resurrection and the appearance of the gospels in print. In sum, I'm comfortable using the apostles' writings as valid representations of Jesus' words and actions.

My second necessary clarification is the answer to a simple question: What led me to qualify something as a theme? I began by writing down thoughts about each passage containing a quote from Jesus or describing His actions. I read and re-read both the verses and my thoughts to identify "big ideas." My only bottom line was that these ideas required support from each of the four gospels. In the end, seven themes emerged. Six of these should be evident in the lives of Christians pursuing Christ's likeness. The seventh, listed as my first theme below, should be a life-altering realization. I like to think of these themes as "practice drills" as we work to play our position.

Theme 1: Jesus Has Authority

This was the final "big idea" to make my list, but I purposely mention it first. While other themes provide life guidance, Jesus' authority inspires awe and reverence. His authority should be stage-setting for the Christian life—Christians must know and acknowledge whom they claim to follow.

Synonyms for authority include *power, control,* and *command.* Throughout the gospels Jesus' authority over the natural world is abundantly evident in miracles and healings. He feeds the thousands (Matt 14:16–21), heals the infirmed or possessed (Matt 8:3; Mark 1:25; Luke 4:35; John 5:6–11), raises the dead (Luke 7:11–17), calms the storm (Mark 4:35–41), walks on water (Matt 14:22–27), alters the disciples' catch (John 21:6), and personally experiences resurrection (Matt 28:5–7; Mark 16:6–7; Luke 24:2–7; John 20:11–14). Furthermore, in all four gospels Jesus acknowledges His role as the Son of Man (Dan 7:13) and, in doing so, claims God-given authority and eternal dominion over all—oneness with God.

In sum, Jesus is no regular traveling teacher with a quick wit and sage advice. Jesus is God's son, part of the Triune God. He has authority over creation. I'll be honest, this truth is both comforting and unsettling—encouraging in that I can live my life knowing the Creator of the universe is available to me at the asking, and disquieting in the sheer magnitude of that thought. At the very least, Jesus' authority is humbling.

So how does Jesus' authority inform the Christian life? First, it gives birth to a reflective expression of faith. Too often individual Christians and the larger body of Christ forget who we are dealing with. We "worship" without thought—"mail it in" so to speak. We walk through traditions and sacraments without intentionality, without remembering whom these events honor. The active knowledge of Jesus' authority should make worship both reverent and authentic. Second, as Christians we frequently envision ourselves as essential cogs in God's plans and therefore attribute God's success to our efforts. Let's face it, God does not need us. He is fully capable of anything without our involvement. That said, He seeks our fellowship. He chooses to use us. Jesus' authority and partnership should make Christians confident with respect to what can happen when He directs our efforts. That is, all things are possible.

Finally, I think the theme of Jesus' authority should be at the forefront of Christians' daily thoughts. We should take time to realize a connection to something much larger than ourselves—to revel in the privilege of God's presence at all times through Christ. Contemporary Christian musician Chris Tomlin says it best in his song *Whom Shall I Fear*:

> I know who goes before me,
> I know who stands behind,
> the God of Angel armies is always by my side;
> The One who reigns forever,
> He is a friend of mine,
> the God of angel armies is always by my side.[1]

Recognizing and submitting to Jesus' authority is, in baseball terms, what "warms me up" each day—what readies me for the game. I only play well when I defer to Him.

Theme 2: Jesus Cares; Jesus Responds

There is significant evidence for this theme in the gospels. Jesus traveled the countryside by foot during His ministry, covering hundreds of miles and meeting thousands of people. The crowds he attracted grew larger and larger. They wanted to be close, to hear and see Him.

This "star" quality is not new to us. Today's political figures, actors, athletes, and the rich and famous all generate crowds and excitement simply by their presence. What was so special about the Jesus phenomenon? He cared. Countless times Jesus stopped during His travels to be present for those in need. Jesus was the poster child for today's "mindfulness" or "intentional living." He heard the desperate cries of parents (Matt 15:22–28) and loved ones (Matt 8:5–13), and touched the most marginalized of society—those with disease, disability, and deformity (Mark 1:40–42; Mark 3:3–5). He was even present when needs were unspoken—for the woman who touched his cloak for healing (Luke 8:43–4) and the woman at the well (John 4:7–15). Jesus was there for everyone, Jew or Gentile (Matt 15:22–28), rich or poor (Mark 10:21–25), male or female (Luke 10:38–42). I'm not sure we get just how big a deal this was. Religious leaders of Jesus' day just were not that available—they would have considered availability beneath their station.

It is one thing to care, and another to respond. Jesus responded by acting in every situation. He healed, fed, and comforted. He raised the dead. Think about this: Jesus took the time to care for and respond to everyone

---

1. "Whom Shall I Fear," lyrics by Chris Tomlin (Burning Lights Album), 2012, Sixteps, Sparrow.

in His path. As much as anything, this illustrates the love of Christ. More than anyone in recorded history, Jesus played his position. He continues to do so today.

How should the theme of caring and responding affect the Christian life? These actions should be our "go-to" responses. Our default behaviors in every relationship should reflect caring and responding. In recent years, I've heard the term "path people" used to describe the aspirational goal of being present for others—meeting the needs of those in front of us. Christians have been encouraged to be path people. How are we doing?

Being present is such a challenge. Our lives seem filled with critical minutia, things so important that we don't have time to stop, to be reflective. This is a real problem for me. I was raised to value a serious work ethic and to respect that ethic in others. All of my life I've felt pressure to never be idle, to always move to the next thing. I fear I've even shared this ethic with my children as life advice. While my "go, go, go" mindset has contributed to professional success and kept me on my path, it has frequently taken me off the path of others. Too often, I've ducked path encounters to avoid being mired in caring and responding.

When my faith was more compartmentalized, I found it easy to care and respond corporately. I could care and occasionally respond through my church with a financial gift or an offer to pray. In other words, I could be a part of a collective caring and responding body. Don't misunderstand here: Corporate caring and responding is a good thing, but it got me off the hook as an individual. It allowed me to avoid those on my personal path too often.

What is the answer? I'm not sure. In my life, being more caring and responsive has been a byproduct of seeking a more intentional walk with Christ. As I make a daily effort to draw closer, to experience His presence, staying on the path with others has become more important. I still fail. Every day I fail. I become absorbed in life and neglect God-given opportunities. My path presence is a work in progress.

Theme 3: Jesus Is Authentic

Synonyms for *authentic* include *genuine*, *real*, and *credible*. Although authenticity is generally considered a positive attribute, being authentic comes with risks. Authenticity requires emotional transparency and can lead to vulnerability. Vulnerability, in turn, is too often perceived as weakness. I think it is safe to say that authenticity is at least in a grey category when considering the world's view of desirable personal traits.

In all four gospels, Jesus is authentic. He cries (John 11:35), becomes frustrated (Luke 9:37–41), shows irritation (Matt 15:25–28), and grows angry (Matt 21:12-13). He loves (John 15:13), appreciates heartfelt adoration (Matt 26:7–12), shows wit and irony (Matt 22:19–21), and relishes the company of children (Matt 19:14). Jesus even expresses apprehension in the face of impending death (Luke 22:42). This all sounds human to me. Throughout His life, Jesus, the son of God, experiences and embraces a wide range of human emotions. And yet, He is God.

I believe Jesus' authenticity is a critical part of His caring and responsiveness. When I am the most real with others, I am in the best place to care and respond. It is as if authenticity heightens my ability to recognize others' needs and possibly even attracts some to my path. If this is the case, why aren't we authentic more often? I think we fear vulnerability. We worry that others may see us as too real, fragile, or broken.

Can authenticity inform Christian living? I think so. In fact, authenticity may be the critical catalytic agent for the successful path person—someone ready to care and respond. Today it seems that too many Christians are anything but real. They supplant piety and claims of righteousness for authenticity. While I'm all about striving to be righteous, I believe an aura of superiority does little to advance the Christian faith. In fact, piety easily leads us down a path to meanness. Unfortunately, today's church too often feeds the piety frenzy. Spiritual leaders emphasize rules and "holy" living at the expense of authenticity. I remember once seeing a bumper sticker that said "God said it, I believe it, that settles it." Well, when it comes to being authentic, our new catch phrase could be "Jesus lived it, and we should too."

Theme 4: Jesus' Values Are Not Shared by This World

In twenty-first-century America, we are driven. We push relentlessly to make money, live big, and have the latest and greatest. Immediate gratification rules. We seek positions of power and authority and bask in the spotlight, especially when it shines directly on us. We value professional attainment regardless of its costs to our family, health, time, or faith. We pride ourselves in self-sufficiency, our ability to store wealth and assure security. We value a narrowly defined beauty seeking youth and bodily perfection until we look out of place. Those challenged to keep pace in our society are scorned for their insufficient discipline and lack of motivation.

Every source of media blares our values of greed and power. Messages tell us to buy the best, to upgrade constantly, and never, never, to be satisfied. We envy those who have what eludes us, and we push to keep pace to the point of exhaustion.

To make matters worse, we live in a throwaway society with an in-the-moment mentality. For some, reusing and recycling are values that betray our God-given dominion over this world and all its assets and inhabitants. After all, we are top dog. If resources serve our purposes today, we care little about what their use costs future generations.

To sum things up, we worship at the altars of wealth, pride, wholeness, outward perfection, immediacy, and the mainstream. People that don't fit, don't belong. They are marginalized, belittled, and forgotten.

What does Jesus value? Let me give you a hint from the world of baseball—we're way off base. To start, Jesus values selflessness and humility (Matt 20:16). He warns that those who seek positions of authority and importance receive rewards only in the here and now. He teaches us that the last are first in His kingdom.

This is a tough pill to swallow. The recent prevailing national message has been loud and clear. We need to be great—we must serve our national interests ahead of the interests of others. We need walls to protect us. It is worth noting that most people we hope to exclude or ignore are considerably less fortunate than we are. They are the "least of these" (Matt 25:40). The call to selflessness and humility is difficult, but a message we must hear. Hold on—it doesn't get easier.

Jesus values love, compassion, and kindness (Mark 12:31; Luke 6:27–28). We're on safe ground now, right? Of course, we love our family and friends; we're compassionate and kind to those we know and trust. With Jesus, however, it goes much deeper. Not once does He say to love only people who look like you, worship as you do, share your perspective, or love like you. He doesn't withhold compassion or kindness from the "undeserving" or those who should be able to help themselves. Jesus' message is simple: Love everyone, be kind to all, extend compassion universally. Nowhere is this call more apparent than in His parable of the Good Samaritan. Here a despised foreigner demonstrates love, compassion, and kindness while others pass by. As a nation and as individuals, we pass by much too often.

Jesus values faith (Luke 17:6). He clearly recognizes and rewards the faith of those he meets. During "Jesus encounters," faith results in healings and wholeness (Mark 5:34; Mark 10: 52). Faith can be defined as belief without clear proof. What makes faith so difficult for us today?

We live in an age that needs proof, a time of "scientific enlightenment." It would be a stretch to say that I'm a scientist, but I have to admit, as a teacher and clinician I value proof. For example, I don't want to teach things that aren't established facts. Likewise, as a clinician, I need to know my therapeutic methods have been proven effective before I use or recommend them. Some have argued that our need for proof, our enlightened perspective, makes faith impossible. I have to admit that I've struggled with this.

During a recent drive through Atlanta, I distracted myself from the terrors of bumper-to-bumper seventy-mile-per-hour traffic with talk radio. Naomi Oreskes, a Harvard professor who studies the history of science, was the interviewee, in a show featuring a compilation of TED talks on scientific inquiry.[2] Eventually, the interview came to the topic of faith. The program host predictably waded into a discussion of the incompatibility of faith and science. To my surprise, Dr. Oreskes suggested that even the most ardent scientists have faith. She elaborated that science has evolved into myriad subspecialties and that no one has universal scientific expertise. For example, a physicist does not necessarily understand biology. Therefore, a physicist may only be able to accept by faith (belief without proofs they understand) complex biological research discoveries. I found this fascinating and shared it with my wife, who extended the argument. She noted that we have faith in doctors, bus drivers, teachers, and farmers, among others, without truly knowing their competence—without proof. Faith, then, seems to be a necessary human behavior. It helps us accept natural phenomena we can't explain and allows us to feel safe in an uncertain world. Yet, when it comes to God, why does faith seem so difficult?

I think it's because faith in God takes us out of the picture. When we have faith, we have to trust in something beyond ourselves—we are no longer *the* authority, *the* agents of knowledge or change. Was this what Jesus was looking for when He called for faith? Is it possible that He wanted His followers to drop the reins of their lives and simply trust in their Creator? I think so.

2. Naomi Oreskes, "Why We Should Trust Scientists," filmed May 2014, TED video, 19:14, https://www.ted.com/talks/naomi_oreskes_why_we_should_believe_in_science.

How should Jesus' values influence Christianity? Let's consider each of the values mentioned above. Individually, Christians must consider honestly if their lives reflect selflessness and humility. Who are we serving, self or others? This type of reflection is painful. In the introduction, I described the Christian life as a cathartic and uncomfortable journey. If this is not true for the individual Christian, maybe life adjustments are necessary. What about selflessness and humility in the larger body of Christ? Too often, I see churches that are inwardly focused—again, serving self. Critical and prayerful introspection by communities of faith should result in a corporate heart for others.

What about love, compassion, and kindness? If individual Christians don't exhibit these values, they are not living like Jesus. Again, I realize that the Christian life is a journey—a life that *always* shows love, compassion, and kindness can seem unachievable. This said, don't be disheartened by your failures. Remember, as Christians, we have grace.

Love, compassion, and kindness should be the first values that come to mind when the corporate body of Christ is mentioned. Churches should be welcoming places, inclusive communities that don't condemn. Remember, we are not in the judgment business. When there is the need for corrective instruction in the corporate body of Christ, Jesus provides specific instructions about how it should occur—initially in private (Matt 18:15–17). I will share much more about the individual and corporate need for love, compassion, and kindness in Chapter 3.

Finally, how should faith inform Christian living? This takes us back to theme 1—Jesus' authority. Faith becomes easier, both individually and corporately, if we acknowledge and act under His authority. That is, if we recognize whom we are dealing with, let God have control, and accept outcomes as part of His broader plan. This is not easy. I've experienced loss and disappointment that appeared senseless, and in these times I felt angry, even a little abandoned. In these situations, I've tried to step back to look at the very big picture. I have a Creator who is simply beyond my comprehension. I am incapable of seeing as He does. I just have to believe (with a history of proof) that He loves me—that all things work together "for the good of those who love him, who have been called according to his purpose" (Rom 8:28).

In sum, adopting the values of Jesus is a tall order. It requires paradigm shifts that flow counter to prevailing culture. It may seem daunting—even impossible. Let's try to simplify things, then. Play your position. Make conscious, daily decisions that reflect Jesus and His values. Big life changes often start with small actions. Remember, He is there as your guide.

Theme 5: Jesus Sets a High Bar for Living

Many of us find comfort in a prescriptive life, where we are told exactly what to do. This black-and-white existence is safe. With respect to our expression of the faith, being black-and-white provides clarity—you know when you are right and when you are wrong. The religious leaders of Jesus' day might have been some of the most prescriptive rule-followers in history. They knew Biblical laws and admonitions by heart and even added to Old Testament commandments by creating a host of additional guidelines for righteous living.

Religious leaders, however, failed to grasp the spirit of God's law. On numerous occasions, they attempted to cast Jesus as a rule-breaker, accusing Him of healing (Matt 12:10–11) and harvesting on the Sabbath (Mark 2:23–27), and of eating prohibited foods (Mark 7:1–5). His responses are consistent with a concept of godliness centered in the here and now. Jesus suggests that when doing God's work, adhering to arbitrary rules is less important than meeting immediate needs, caring, and responding. In Matt 15:7, Jesus goes further, accusing authorities of "breaking the commands of God" for the sake of traditions. He notes that their hearts were far from God and that their worship was in vain. Simply stated, these leaders were legalistic in their compliance with God, while Jesus complied pragmatically and completely.

Possibly no New Testament passage illustrates Jesus' high bar more than the Sermon on the Mount (Matt 5:21–22; 27–30). He warns that anger as well as murder is unacceptable, and that we should not only avoid adultery but also impure thoughts. Jesus even suggests that we should live without parts of our bodies if they cause us to sin. This more extreme message conveys the seriousness of His call. In a word, it is less about the letter of the law and more about the intent of the heart.

Finally, Jesus gives us a very clear guide to the "high bar" life when asked which commandments are most important. He responds, "Love the Lord your God with all your heart and with all your soul and with all your strength and with all your mind and, love your neighbor as yourself" (Luke 10:27). Jesus knows that loving God completely will change the intent of our hearts. He also knows that the call to love others as we love ourselves brings home His message. Jesus' answer provides both a heavenly and a human context for our actions.

How should Jesus' high bar affect the Christian life? It convicts those of us who think we're where we need to be in this life. If we are honest, no one can claim to meet His standards. But there is more. Jesus' high bar is inspirational. Few people achieve remarkable things without setting lofty goals. Jesus sets the bar high to provide us, individually and collectively, with distant targets. He knows that too often we settle, content with "good enough" in our Christian walks. But Jesus calls us to push the limits like fine-tuned athletes, to live as He did. For the individual Christian and the corporate body of Christ, this is lifelong work that transforms followers to His image. In my life, there has been little I've appreciated more than to be told I'm like my earthly father. He was an amazing man. Jesus wants us to strive to be like Him, the perfect image-bearer of our Heavenly Father. Realizing the magnitude of that goal, He provides us with His presence as we try and with His grace when we fail.

Theme 6: Jesus Shows Indignation

Finally, a theme we can embrace! We all get mad. The fact that Jesus did provides some measure of comfort, right? Before you get too excited, consider a few things. First, what is indignation?

Indignation is anger caused by injustice. The term "righteous indignation" goes a bit farther, suggesting that indignant people are guilt-free and therefore their anger is just. In my review of the canonical gospels, Jesus showed righteous indignation. He rebuked trickery and hardheartedness (Matt 24:24) and overturned money changers in the temple (John 2:15). Jesus bristled at hypocrisy (Matt 23:2–7), pride (Luke 18:10–14), greed (Luke 12:15), and indifference (Matt 13:15).

You may say, "Bill, I'm still feeling pretty good; my indignation is righteous." Good for you; mine is often anything but. I get angry at my animals when they annoy me, the traffic when it crowds me, my wife when she leaves vegetable peelings in the sink, and my kids when they change the television channel. This illustrates my second point about Jesus' indignation—unlike for me, it wasn't His go-to response. Recall that a few pages ago, I suggested caring and responding fit that bill. Now, can you honestly say your anger is righteous?

How should Jesus' indignation instruct the Christian walk? It is like crossing an old wooden bridge. The kind that creaks and bows with each step—that is missing a few critical boards here and there. Like walking on that old rotting bridge, when we become indignant we are always one careless step from disaster. Too often, what begins as justified frustration or anger grows to simple judgment. You know my take on judgment—it's not our job.

Should the righteous ire of Christians be evident in today's world? One would think so given the widespread presence of injustice, poverty, discrimination, and violence; the destruction of our planet; the growing plight of refugees. It is shameful that these obvious wrongs appear to matter so little to many professing Christians. This may be due to the compartmentalization I came to acknowledge in my own life. If our lives are pursued with blinders on and in well-defined boxes, the plight of others and our world may be difficult to perceive. We may struggle to see beyond our own needs and circumstances. Christians must also consider the possibility that our frequent lack of concern with human tragedy may result from preoccupation with a legalistic faith. We may be too busy judging others—their lifestyles and their choices—to show righteous indignation when and where it is needed.

Finally, I believe it is time for the corporate body of Christ, His church, to show righteous indignation in regard to the inequalities and injustices mentioned above. This must occur, however, without judgment and as a call to action. Simply put, the pain of this world provides vast chances for caring and responding. As the body of Christ, we need leaders who help us identify opportunities to be like Jesus, who lead using Christ's example as their guide.

Theme 7: Jesus Says, "Follow Me"

This last theme calls us to play our position: *to emulate Christ.* Jesus uses the phrase "follow me" twenty-three times in the New Testament. I think He was trying to tell us something.

Why do we follow? Following becomes necessary when we are off course. I don't know how many times I have followed others when I was, or feared becoming, lost. Now, GPS is almost a household guiding device, but even it is not 100% reliable.

We also follow others when they offer something we value—something we want to imitate. This kind of following can be cathartic. Remember, however, the character of those we follow steers the direction of our potential life change. In history, there have been charismatic, evil leaders that led devoted followers down dark paths. We need to show discernment when choosing whom we follow.

Why not follow Jesus? I've pointed to admirable attributes (my themes) that suggest His example is worth following. I've also identified Jesus as God's son, a claim that, if true, gives His followers access to His ultimate authority. I realize that there are countless religions that value many of the themes I've shared in this chapter. In no way do I sit in judgment of those pursuing these faiths. This said, I would be remiss, if not irresponsible, if I did not identify Jesus as someone worth following for those looking for direction. My father often told me that a prayerful and open-minded reading of John's gospel could be an entry point for those interested in pursuing Christ. Let me encourage seekers to consider that path.

How should Jesus' call to "follow Me" inform the Christian faith? In every way. If we choose to follow Him, we must emulate Him. His call to follow is our call to caring and responding; to authenticity; to the values of selflessness, humility, love, compassion, kindness, and faith; to an aspirational "high bar" life; and to righteous indignation in response to this world's unfairness.

I'm reminded of the Jackie DeShannon song "Put a Little Love in Your Heart."[3] The lyrics admonish us to help our fellow man—to put love in our hearts. It has been my experience that following Jesus, though challenging and often uncomfortable, puts His love in your heart. It changes you. The love of Christ reorients your priorities. It puts God first, others second, and ourselves last.

Ideally, the themes I have mentioned should coalesce in the lives of Christians. What does this look like? As I close this chapter, I share my perceptions of two Christian lives I've had the profound privilege of observing over the past twenty-six years. Hopefully, the following portrayals will animate my themes. Let me introduce Elaine and Jack.

I met Elaine seven years ago when our family became affiliated with my in-laws' church. After settling into regular attendance at the more casual worship service, I began to play guitar with the worship band. Each

---

3. "Put a Little Love in Your Heart," Lyrics by Jackie De Shannon, Randy Myers, and Jimmy Holiday (1969), Imperial Records.

Sunday, worship began as the band played and the congregation mingled in a welcoming fashion. From my perch up front, I consistently observed one thing. Elaine, in a very unassuming way, working the sanctuary, finding those who were alone or first-time visitors, spending a few moments to ask about their lives or to offer an encouraging word.

As the weeks passed, my wife and I joined Elaine's Sunday School class. During prayer requests, she listened quietly while writing in her prayer journal. As class members offered concerns, her eyes locked with theirs, revealing an intentional presence I envied. When Elaine chose to speak, everyone listened. You see, she commanded considerable respect. The more I learned of her life, the more I understood why.

What I came to appreciate most about Elaine was her ability to find my path at opportune times. She asked about my aging mother or my children when my concerns were heightened. Elaine had a God-given knack to be there when I needed reassurance and prayer, to always say the right thing.

Initially unknown to me, Elaine was a quiet force of caring and responding in my community. Behind the scenes, she consistently marshaled and directed resources to meet local needs. Her primary focus was "the least of these"—individuals and families suffering from financial misfortune or spiraling life choices.

Elaine served tirelessly in local agencies providing others access to food, clothing, and shelter. She also maintained central roles in several service arms of our church. All of this said, Elaine found her special niche at Christmas. For twenty-six years, she collected money and gifts for children in poverty. What began as a modest endeavor, serving about fifty local families, is now a regional holiday response to over a thousand households.

Last year Elaine resigned from her role as the local "Christmas Coordinator" to be more available for her family. Interestingly, Elaine's husband told me that this past Christmas she could not remain idle. To the contrary, Elaine was a central force in gift collections for over one hundred local migrant farm workers and their families.

I met Jack soon after our family moved to western North Carolina. A big, barrel-chested man, Jack's greetings began with an asymmetrical smile and a twinkling eye. In my church community, Jack was unassuming but ever-present. Like Elaine, he lived the life of a servant. I can see him now, apron-adorned, cooking for the town's "Poor Man's Lunch," or standing in the parking lot offering aid to a stranded passer-by, or simply putting his arm around a hurting friend. Jack's real talent was with construction. I have fond memories of hurricane-relief trips where I provided the labor (the lifting and shoveling), while Jack, and others like him, masterfully did the skilled carpentry.

Like Elaine, Jack had a God sense—that special availability to others. He also shared Elaine's ability to be present regardless of his commitments or schedule; his priorities were right.

Jack disdained the spotlight. He never sought attention for his actions. Jack just kept his ear to the tracks, and cared and responded. He needed no credit. This was just who Jack was.

Once in passing I mentioned to Jack that the railing on my back deck was rotting. Remember, I am not a fixer; I'm a laborer. Jack had worked with me and knew this repair was well over my head. I came home late one afternoon to the sounds of boards dropping and a power saw cutting. In my backyard, I saw Jack replacing my railing. He took nothing for it and assured me it was no trouble. Jack died of a massive heart attack a few days later. There will never be a way to measure Jack's impact on our community, his quiet responses to the needs of others.

I bet you know people like Elaine and Jack—individuals emulating Christ every day. People caring and responding with authenticity; living their values of selflessness, humility, love, compassion, kindness, and faith; holding a high bar for their life that encourages their best while keeping them humble; playing their position while following Jesus. My guess is that the Christian Elaines and Jacks of this world do what they do because they have been changed through a personal encounter with Jesus. They know and submit to His authority.

Unfortunately, many claiming the name of Christ too often show a dark side inconsistent with Jesus and the themes that characterize His life. The meanness they express in His name stains the body of Christ, making Christianity unappealing, if not off-putting. As we shift our attention to mean Christianity, remember the themes presented in this chapter and that they appear in the lives of so many. Countless people out there are playing their position—not error-free, but nonetheless playing every day—striving to be closer and closer to Christ's likeness.

CHAPTER 3

What Is Mean Christianity?

In the business world, branding rules. Successful marketing depends upon brands that appeal to consumers. A brand is the "lived experience" of a product—what our collective involvement with merchandise tells us about its core nature, qualities, and appeal. Branding results from both personal product experiences and our general and passing product perceptions. It influences spending in that we buy what we experience or perceive to be of value.

What is the "Christian" brand today, the lived experiences and perceptions of those who walk with Christians daily? Does this brand mirror the values of Jesus? Are Christians viewed as selfless, humble, compassionate, loving, and kind—as authentic, caring, and responding—even as indignant in response to this world's injustice? Is our world experiencing and perceiving a brand worth buying? These are all serious questions for the body of Christ.

Before examining mean Christianity, I must share that I encounter Christlike Christians daily. Followers like Elaine and Jack (Chapter 2), who live like Jesus. These people play their position and, in doing so, do their part to enhance the Christian brand. Like me, they fail (we all do) but continue on by His grace.

Unfortunately, too many other Christians defame the brand by living in ways that not only fail the Christlike litmus test, but also turn others away from the possibility of following Jesus. Impeding individuals from following Christ is simply not acceptable. In Matt 18:6, Jesus' words are much stronger than mine: "If anyone causes one of these little ones—those who believe in me—to stumble, it would be better for them to have a large millstone hung around their neck and to be drowned in the depths of the sea." Let's face it, obstructing the possible faith of others is a serious offense, one that, in baseball terms, "gets you thrown out of the game." Is it possible that the actions of Christians cause people to stumble—to fail to consider the faith or to perceive it negatively?

I know some readers are saying, "Bill, you're making a mountain of a molehill. There are folks out there who make Christians look bad, but not many, right?" Recently, I ran a few quick Google searches to take the pulse of negative perceptions of Christianity. I started by entering two words: "angry Christians." To my surprise, there were over fourteen million hits. I followed this with "petty Christians" and "selfish Christians." Each search resulted in about 700,000 hits. The words "despicable Christians" resulted in almost a half million hits. Admittedly, some responses to my search efforts were instructive warnings against these traits; however, the vast majority were less-than-flattering accounts of individual Christians or the body of Christ. Is it possible that mean Christianity is real? I think so.

Too often the body of Christ doesn't see the meanness it promotes. I'll give you an example. A few Christian friends read portions of this book when it was in draft form. I'm not the strongest editor, so I hoped multiple sets of eyes would catch mistakes. Of course, I also sought insights and suggestions. One or two offered a surprising and curious reaction. The title, *Mean Christianity*, did not resonate with their experiences. They just didn't relate to meanness as a problem for Christians. Their reaction was very inconsistent with my Google search results. Is it possible that some in the body of Christ are unaware of this issue? Whether we see it or not, many in today's world feel anything but loved by God's people.

The disconnect between Christians and mean Christianity is a critical point. In baseball terms, you can't hit what you can't see. Accordingly, we need to clarify mean Christianity—to deconstruct it in a way that allows the body of Christ to take a more critical look at itself. Only in doing so can Christians evaluate the costs of their actions and experience the changes of heart needed to promote a Christlike brand.

When used as an adjective, synonyms for *mean* include *nasty, offensive, selfish, petty, contemptible,* and *despicable.* I see you shaking your head, saying, "Come on Bill, Christians who are nasty or despicable? Really?" I honestly think that the majority of Christians don't consistently act this way. Some, however, do.

As I have said, we can't hit what we can't see, so let's consolidate it all into a definition of mean Christianity. A mean Christian claims Christ yet, at least some of the time, treats others in petty, offensive, or despicable ways. Selfishness may also motivate mean Christianity. Furthermore, a mean Christian may feel that their actions are justified, that their meanness is righteous (more on this in Chapter 4). As with my definition of Christianity in Chapter 2, mean Christianity occurs at both individual and corporate levels. A little later in this chapter, I will offer illustrative examples of meanness within the body of Christ and individual Christians. I discuss these examples not to judge the Christians involved but to make a point, to address our disconnect with this topic. Before we move to examples, there are two questions to answer.

First, is mean Christianity new? Heavens no. Mean Christianity has been around since the early church. In his epistle, James chastises early Christian ministers for neglecting the needs of the poor to assist others with creating wealth (Jas 2:1–7). He also identifies the problem of careless talk (gossip) among believers (Jas 3:5–6). At the same time, it is important to note that the early Christian church was also depicted quite positively. In the second chapter of Acts, Paul characterizes early Christians as learning and growing in the faith, encouraging fellowship, demonstrating extreme generosity, praying constantly, and showing joy and gladness. In sum, most early Christians seemed to be living like Jesus.

In the first millennium of the faith, Christian meanness surfaced as violence against nonbelievers. Angry Christian mobs destroyed pagan temples, killed pagan priests, and brutally murdered philosophers.[1] When he was King of the Franks, Charlemagne killed thousands who were unwilling to convert, while the church sanctioned the killing of thousands more who refused to pay religious taxes.[2]

During the early part of the second millennium, crusades resulted in the deaths of tens of thousands in the name of Christ.[3] The centuries that

1. Ramsay McMullen, *Christianizing the Roman Empire: A.D.100–400* (New Haven, CT: Yale University Press, 1984).

2. Alessandro Barbero, *Charlemagne: Father of a Continent* (Oakland, CA: University of California Press, 2004).

3. Jonathan Phillips, "The Crusades: A Complete History," *History Today* 65, no. 5 (May 2015), http://www.historytoday.com/jonathan-phillips/crusades-complete-history.

followed saw "heretics" (often those raising legitimate questions about the faith) harassed and murdered.[4]

Modern times offer more examples of mean Christianity. The history of Jim Crow in the United States is replete with Christians' justifications of heinous acts against African Americans.[5] Furthermore, early land grabs and relocations specific to America's indigenous peoples often occurred simultaneously with Christian missionary efforts.[6] On a more global scale, Hitler's attempts to eradicate European Jews met with only tacit resistance from many German Christians. Today, the Catholic church's global leadership continues to face harsh criticism for its lack of a strong stance against the World War II–era German regime.[7]

In the past fifty years (and before), violence and discrimination have been perpetrated against people of color by those self-identifying as Christians. Most recently, a worldwide contempt for immigrants has occurred to the satisfaction of some in the Christian community and without objection by others. It must be said, however, that many Christians have spoken out on behalf of immigrants and refugees.

So, mean Christianity is not new. It's been with us since the inception of the faith. Why worry about it now? What is different about mean Christianity today?

Two things come to mind. First, there has been a recent groundswell of meanness unleashed by the emergence and sanctioning of an "anything goes" mentality. As a Southerner who grew up in a different era, I am amazed by what I see and hear these days. Strong words and emotions in passing conversations make me blush. Television shows and movies push the boundaries of decency. Actions heretofore unseen and unspoken have become the norm. As lines blur between acceptable and unacceptable behavior, we all feel freer to speak emotionally, act before thinking, and even be mean.

4. Edward J. Watts, *City and School in Late Antique Athens and Alexandria* (Oakland, CA: University of California Press, 2006).

5. Jamelle Bouie, "Christian Soldiers: The Lynching and Torture of Blacks in the Jim Crow South Weren't Just Acts of Racism. They Were Religious Rituals," *Slate*, February 10, 2015, http://www.slate.com/articles/news_and_politics/politics/2015/02/jim_crow_south_s_lynching_of_blacks_and_christianity_the_terror_inflicted.html.

6. "Atrocities Against Native Americans," United End to Genocide, http://endgenocide.org/learn/past-genocides/native-americans.

7. John Cornwell, *Hitler's Pope: The Secret History of Pius the XII* (New York: Viking Press, 1999).

Our recent political climate offered brazen, callous behavior as a formula for winning. Crass, offensive, and hurtful language became the rule. Crowds were whipped into a frenzy with spiteful rhetoric. When individuals holding positions of authority model meanness, they legitimize it for society as a whole.

What else is different about meanness today? You have heard "What happens in Vegas, stays in Vegas." Not true. Anything and everything that happens today is easily known by others. In the age of the internet and social media, nothing is hidden. People share obscure "selfies," post photographs of their meals with others, blog about the most mundane aspects of their lives, and spend much of their time reading the social media posts of others. As we have become tied to our smartphones and addicted to media feeds, meanness has taken on new life. The anonymity of the keyboard has encouraged voices from our darker sides. The smallest of offenses or comments, when offered via a social media platform, can become divisive and snowball into ugliness. While one might think that social media use by Christians would illustrate and advocate for the values of Christ, too often this is anything but true. A simple search of the internet reveals mean posts, blogs, and newsfeeds originating from self-identifying Christians and Christian organizations.

I'm confident that the entire body of Christ—the worldwide church— does not consistently act or speak in a mean or unkind manner. But if enough Christians are or can be mean, we have a problem. To use a baseball analogy, when one player gets thrown out for stealing a base, the entire team may lose their opportunity to bat. Simply put, the body of Christ must identify and speak out against meanness. The costs of not doing so are too high.

From this point forward, I will discuss illustrative examples of mean Christianity. Corporate cases are considered first, followed by individual examples. My stories have been selected from print and online media, as well as from personal experiences and from the experiences of those close to me.

CORPORATE CHRISTIAN MEANNESS

I'll start with a dramatic example highlighted in a *USA Today* report on March 21, 2014.[8] The story described the origins and actions of Westboro

8. Lindsay Deutsch, "Five Incendiary Westboro Baptist Church Funeral Protests," *USA*

Baptist Church (WBC) in Topeka, Kansas. WBC was founded in 1955 by Fred Phelps and is best known for its strong stance against homosexuality. To express their belief that homosexuals are an "abomination" and the root of God's anger against America, church supporters have picketed at countless events, including prominent funerals of soldiers and those killed by gun violence. Signs displayed offer phrases like "Thank God for Dead Soldiers," "Too Late to Pray," and "Thank God for 9/11." The church website displays the tagline, "God Hates Fags," and offers a narrative explaining church positions and links to video and audio resources with titles like "Christians Caused Fag Marriage" and "God Hates Your Prayers."

I bet most readers will give me this one. That is, you will at least agree that the tactics of WBC are mean. So mean, in fact, that numerous faith-based and secular groups have responded with counter-protests to disrupt WBC picketing events. WBC's tactics are mean enough to earn a "hate group" designation by the Southern Poverty Law Center.[9]

The behaviors of WBC are blatantly inconsistent with the themes of Christlike living I described in Chapter 2. They are offensive, despicable, and misguided. And, incredibly, they are exhibited by individuals claiming Christianity.

Why would Christians drift so far off base? I don't know. My guess is WBC members and associates are trying to attract attention through the extreme nature of their actions. I can only assume that they feel a responsibility to point out what they perceive as the wrongdoing of others. I can further assume that they see themselves as doing "God's bidding."

I've been to baseball games in which players or coaches raised their voices and even became violent over an umpire's call or an opposing team's actions. While this attracted attention, it was negative attention and the behavior frequently resulted in poor individual or team play. In my life, I have never been convinced by unkind words or actions to adopt ideas or positions. To the contrary, I listen better and respond more completely when others make an effort to connect—to know and even care for me.

Before moving on, I'd be remiss if I did not point out that highly visible examples of meanness (or for that matter, any example) may be the only things some non-Christians ever experience about the faith. Think of the

---

Today, March 21, 2014, https://www.usatoday.com/story/news/nation-now/2014/03/21/westboro-baptist-church-pickets-funerals/6688951/.

9. Southern Poverty Law Center, "Hate Map," https://www.splcenter.org/hatemap?gclid=EAIaIQobChMI5vmS3Yvo1QIVghaBChob8gsUEAAYAiAAEgIN2_D_BwE. [March 15, 2017]

nonbeliever who only reads of or experiences WBC's brand of Christianity. What will be their lived Christian experience? What will they perceive about Christianity? Will they embrace the faith? Remember Jesus' millstone reference in Matt 18:6. Those exhibiting extreme meanness would do well to consider that obstructing the faith of others does not please Christ.

We'll consider one additional visible example of corporate Christian meanness before moving on to less inflammatory cases. Few issues today are more controversial than immigration. Political parties offer radically different assessments of threats associated with worldwide migration, and the Christian church has not remained silent. In fact, many Christian groups have developed or endorsed inclusive policies, while others have taken strong, negative stands.

The illustration I highlight does not emerge from a specific church body but reflects the thoughts of a broader group claiming Christ. Although I could point to several anti-immigration Christian websites and publications, I'll just mention one Facebook page—"Christians Against Illegal Immigration."[10] While the page states support for legal aliens, it labels illegal immigrants as "thieves," "robbers," and "non-English speakers." It also offers unflattering rhetoric describing immigrants as "stealing American benefits" and "hurting" American workers and interests. The page includes posts that disparage those who hold views other than those shared by the site and warns of diminishing "white" influence.

I know some readers may not be persuaded that this example reflects Christian meanness. Let me clarify that I am not writing to argue about immigration law or its enforcement. I am writing as a Christian concerned about the Christian brand—others' lived experiences and perceptions of Christianity. I believe meanness surfaces in the issue of immigration when people—creations of God—are disparaged. When one group simplifies complex issues to "black and white" or "right and wrong" constructs, it is easy to be mean. Meanness shielded by the comfort of group consensus provides a stimulus for boldness—for saying and doing things we likely would not consider otherwise.

Let's go back to theme 2 from Chapter 2—Jesus Cares; Jesus Responds. My advice for avoiding Christian meanness is simple: Play your position. Care for and respond to everyone God puts in your path. This includes those who don't speak English or share your skin color. If these people

10. Facebook, "Christians Against Illegal Immigration," https://www.facebook.com/enforceimmigrationlaws/. [March 15, 2017]

aren't in your daily paths, consider how to change that. Volunteer with service agencies in your community, or ask others how you can serve. Playing your position with immigrant populations will require you to know these individuals, to see and experience the world as they do. My guess is that being in their path will keep you from succumbing to group stereotypes. It may also allay the meanness that can follow such categorizations. I've found that it is hard for me to be a part of collective meanness when I know and care for individuals within targeted groups.

Let's move our discussion of corporate Christian meanness to the local level. Two examples follow that could be found in most communities. One considers meanness resulting from envy, while the other examines meanness as an artifact of an inward focus.

Corporate Christian meanness can occur when one church envies the accomplishments of another or fears their potential competition. Recently, I asked a pastor friend about corporate meanness, and he conveyed a simple personal story.

After several years as an associate pastor in a larger church, my friend decided to start a new faith community. At some personal and financial risk, he followed God's leading and initiated what became a thriving congregation. My friend's calling was for the unchurched—those who felt uncomfortable in a more formal setting. As his congregation grew, local churches had varied responses to its success. Some offered support and financial assistance, while others envied the success of his new church and feared the competition it presented. My friend recalled several mean actions from this latter group, including negative public comments by prominent Christians in the community and disparaging or condemning website posts. Of course, those offering hurtful remarks discouraged their churches from being a part of this new effort to reach others for Christ.

This reminds me of Little League. I think you probably picked up on the fact that I was no star. I was anything but—remember my earlier comment about praying the ball would not be hit my way. As a habitual second teamer who relied on the "Coach, you gotta play them all" rule, I sat and watched as a handful of talented players received attention. While I was on some good teams and I enjoyed winning, I envied those star players.

Envy is a common human trait that can be destructive, especially in the body of Christ. When we see a church growing in faith and meeting community needs, we should celebrate. We should also offer assistance if, by doing so, we can amplify their impact. Why, then, do we fail to come together and cheer for each other? Sometimes it is differences in religious dogma or even generational divides. I'm not suggesting that as individual churches, we should all do things the same way. I'm simply saying that we shouldn't beat up our brothers and sisters in Christ because they may be doing things differently or "compete" for members. We're all on the same team, right?

Envy is one of those meanness catalysts that pits Christian against Christian. Many who have experienced Christian meanness are fellow believers. It serves us well to note that Christians don't discriminate when it comes to meanness—everyone is a potential target.

My final example of meanness in the corporate Christian body originates from a "those people" mentality. The perception of external groups as "those people" typically emanates from exclusivity, based on factors such as race, ethnicity, gender, sexual orientation, poverty, and even wealth. Whether their meanness is overt or covert, churches where "those people" are excluded do not reflect Christ's likeness.

"Those people" churches may well be inwardly focused or even elite. A "those people" perspective can also emerge from a fear of difference or the unknown. A "those people" mindset licenses us to avoid, discriminate against, defame, and even condemn others. Many times we can fall into "those people" habits. That is, we become comfortable with our church contacts—people we see the most. We may even see no reason to include others. This can be addressed with simple awareness and a caring attitude. There are times, however, when "those people" actions seriously damage the Christian brand.

I'll give you just a few examples from my life. As a child and young adult who grew up in the Deep South, I attended churches in which people of color were "those people." I guess "we" excused "ourselves" by thinking that "they" had "their own" churches, and that "we" would likely be unwelcome there. I vividly remember missionaries of color speaking in our church and being welcomed and even praised for their efforts. The troubling thing was that if these same individuals had walked into a Sunday morning service without their "missionary pass," I'm fairly certain they would have been unwelcome. This reaction might not have been overt, although I can't say this with certainty. I am confident, however, there would have been a "those people" dynamic at work. This is less of the case today. While I am sure there are congregations in the South and elsewhere that discriminate based on race, there are also vibrant and effective integrated churches.

I have a friend who once shared why he was not involved in church. He conveyed the story of a faith community's open rejection of his gay brother. This experience had stayed with my friend for years and had become a barrier preventing his fellowship with other believers. I'm also aware of a situation in which a pastor's openness to all, regardless of their sexual orientation, contributed to his removal and a split in his church that took years to mend.

I'm not debating homosexuality here. Remember, I am not the judge, and the log in my eye is obscenely large. I am, however, stating that it is mean to belittle God's creation. The psalmist said we are beautifully and wonderfully made (Ps 139:14). If the church excludes "those people" from fellowship, it is excluding God's beautiful creation. This is inexcusable. All of us need Christ and the unconditional support of His corporate body.

What about other "those people" groups—the indigent, the poorly dressed, the unattractive, women who feel God's call to service, the transgendered, those of different religious traditions or beliefs? Are these individuals treated as "those people" in your church or in mine? Does the body of Christ (or groups within that body) avoid or ostracize others? Let's face facts. It happens—either as a public church statement or through more back-channel avenues with a tacit "understanding." Recognizing "those people" meanness is the first step to stopping it. We could all benefit from some introspection in this area.

Before turning to individual Christian meanness, I should mention that the corporate examples provided above can certainly occur at the individual level. That is, the extreme tactics of Westboro Baptist Church can be seen in an individual's life. Likewise, an individual can be mean or unwelcoming to an immigrant or hurtful to another Christian they envy. One individual can choose to see another as one of "those people"—someone not worthy of inclusion or grace. I hate to admit that at times during my life, I have been guilty of individual and possibly corporate meanness in most of these areas. The time I've wasted being mean has kept me off the paths of others too often. I hope and pray it has not been an obstacle to their faith. Abandoning meanness in any form requires a prayerful and purposeful relationship with Christ.

INDIVIDUAL CHRISTIAN MEANNESS

Let's look at a few examples of individual Christian meanness. We can start with the one mentioned earlier in this chapter, from the book of James. James rebukes the early church for gossiping (Jas 3:5–6). I think gossip is a fairly universal concept, but for clarity's sake let's just define it as idle talk that may express some truth, some innuendo, and a little exaggeration. Gossip usually has a degree of excitement—excitement that often occurs at the expense of others.

In Chapter 1, I mentioned that I lived the life of Opie Taylor. Of course, Opie was the son of Andy Griffith on *The Andy Griffith Show* in the 1960s. This show, a simple and somewhat ideal portrayal of rural life, has always been one of my favorites. There was an early episode in which Andy (the sheriff and show's star) teases his Aunt Bea about gossiping with her friends. This angers Aunt Bea, who offers a few leading comments about a traveling shoe salesman in the presence of Andy and his deputy, Barney Fife. The episode builds into a hilarious tale as Andy and Barney gossip to a host of interested townspeople (mostly men) about the salesman's real role as a New York talent scout. After the town is well stocked with shoes and exhausted from auditions for the unsuspecting salesman, Andy and the others learn the truth and realize their susceptibility to gossip.

We are all prone to gossip. It takes attention away from our problems. Let's just admit it: Gossiping can be fun. While gossiping may seem harmless, it can have irreparable consequences. A few small and possibly elaborated details can snowball into large-scale falsehoods, marring real people's lives and ending relationships. Is the momentary rush associated with sharing someone else's faults, pain, or disappointments worth these consequences?

I gossip too much. I share things I know carelessly and with little regard for their potential impact on those involved. My dear mother once said, "If you can't say something nice, don't say anything at all." I believe James was telling us to watch our tongues and be intentional about what we say. Have you noticed that the call to an intentional life with Christ keeps surfacing as a solution to meanness?

Two more examples of individual Christian meanness come to mind. I've touched on one already—social media. I grew up in a different time, in an era where communication required significant person-to-person contact. When we actually talked to each other, we were socialized into roles as conversational partners. We learned to "read" others and respond accordingly. When "talking" meant moving our mouths, we took greater care with what we said because there was nowhere to hide. As speakers, we were front and center with our conversational partners.

Today things are different. Sure, we still have face-to-face encounters, but we also increasingly use technology as a communication tool. I'm as guilty as most here. I carry a smartphone almost all the time. I check the internet for scores and news, and yes, reluctantly, I've been drawn into the world of texting.

Technology has made it easy to catch others when we need them. It has also created new platforms for personal and public communication. Facebook is a wonderful example. Almost everyone I know maintains a Facebook presence, sharing the most (and least) interesting details of their lives. Aside from Facebook, there is Snapchat, Instagram, and Periscope, along with countless other social media outlets, as well as blogs that offer a venue for more detailed entries. To my knowledge, all social media opportunities allow for some interaction. That is, others can comment on postings or "like" and "tag" entries.

Of course, as with the corporate meanness example of Westboro Baptist Church, anyone, including Christians, can simply post mean things. Negative entries are bad enough, but the comments following posts can get dicey.

I'm a professor. I like healthy discourse. In fact, I expect my students to engage in a spirited exchange of ideas. Too often, however, things become very ugly on social media. Comments express individual attacks on others and invite additional negative dialogue. Many times individuals identify as Christians first before delving into tirades that do not reflect Jesus. They offer angry rhetoric about people who don't share their faith, who look and live in ways they don't understand or value. Though I'm not a regular on social media, I have encountered self-identified Christians criticizing other Christians' posts—posts that embody a spirit of caring, authenticity, selflessness, humility, love, and compassion.

I think meanness appears in social media because individuals are not face-to-face with their audience. Christians must think before writing. Remember that in Chapter 2, I said being a Christian is living like Jesus all day, every day. This includes those seemingly safe times when we are behind the protection of a keyboard. As Christians we are constantly judged—like it or not, our actions are the only gospel that many will ever experience. We must live intentionally, knowing that we contribute to the broader brand of Christianity.

My final example of individual Christian meanness takes a different twist. I've considered specific mean actions, but now let's focus on meanness in personal priorities. Can what we value in life reflect meanness? Early in this chapter, I pointed out several synonyms for the word *mean*, including *selfish*. Let's just be honest: For most of us, the needs of self are front and center. Selfishness is the elephant in the room that drives many daily decisions.

As a selfish person, I neglect the obvious needs of others to address my personal wants and desires. I'm drawn into our materialistic world, buying things I really don't need. I also too often put myself above others when it comes to time. In sum, I struggle with selfishness.

But I'm not alone. All around me, people are self-serving. We're taught from an early age to ascend the social and financial ladder, to "look out for number one." Unfortunately, selfishness has become a value we all embrace. Remember theme four from Chapter 2? Jesus' values are not shared by this world. While selflessness runs counter to our human nature, Jesus is all about others.

Sadly, there are individuals who simply choose not to see beyond themselves. This intentional blindness toward others often coincides with feelings of superiority. It takes us back to earlier comments about "those people." Christians who are intentionally selfish could benefit from a close examination of the life of Jesus. If they claim Christ's primacy as a central faith tenet, then intentional, willful selfishness is not acceptable.

For others, they see selfishness as deserved. That is, they feel they have earned a right to focus on the self, to amass wealth, to protect their time. This vantage point has an ugly side. That is, the "deserving" often judge "others" for their life circumstances: "They haven't worked hard enough." "They just have to pull themselves up by their bootstraps." Deserved selfishness and intentional selfishness are closely related, but the former often expresses itself in indignation or judgment.

For some, selfishness arises as a result of the compartmentalized life I described earlier—living in neat and separate categories. As we divide and conquer life, we have little time for anything else. Outside of a possible compartment dedicated to faith, we can keep our heads down, plowing through to-do lists and unresponsive to the needs of others.

Finally, selfishness can be more incidental. Unfortunately, many of us don't think of ourselves as selfish, yet our minute-to-minute decisions serve us more than they do others. Suppressing the self requires intentionality. It helps if we value others. Remember, Jesus said to love others as we love ourselves. That mindset contributes to an "other" focus.

Before concluding this chapter, I must consider one more possible expression of Christian meanness—inactivity in the Christian life. For example, corporate or individual inactivity in the presence of need is inconsistent with the life of Christ. This idea may be unpopular and even controversial, but it deserves our attention.

In Chapter 2, I spoke of caring and responding as go-to behaviors for those seeking Christ's likeness. When the body of Christ or individual Christians are aware of others' needs yet fail to act, I believe their inactivity can be perceived by others as willful and mean. I understand that failing to act in the presence of need may simply relate to not knowing what to do or being overwhelmed by the enormity of a task at hand. This said, inaction is not acceptable. It is not Christlike, and it hurts the Christian brand.

I use baseball analogies throughout this book to illustrate points about the Christian faith. For the most part, I think the comparison works. This time it doesn't. In baseball, only nine players per team are on the field during a game. Sure, occasionally you see players charge the field to congratulate a peer on a home run or the final pitch in a shutout, but for the most part, it is nine players playing and another dozen or so watching from the dugout.

In Christianity, unlike in baseball, we never get a break—we're never in the dugout icing our shoulders. We are on the field all the time—the game never ends. Accordingly, when a need arises in our individual paths or in a broader path that we all travel, Christians should be the first to care and respond—not just when it is easy and convenient, but all the time. I've described the life of a Christian as an uncomfortable journey, and being Christ's first responders can certainly make it that way.

Again you may be saying, "Bill, I'm good here. I care and respond. I'm always in the game." But are you really? I'm not. Not for the little things, like my pastor's call for help on Saturdays with community tasks or volunteering to help others. And not for the big things either. Right now there is significant injustice in our world—poverty, violence, lack of heath care, the plight of refugees, the absence of the protection of universal rights. Too often, as a Christian, I sit on my hands. Though upset by drifts in national and international policy away from caring, responding, and inclusiveness, I don't act.

As Christians, moral injustice should be grounds for that righteous indignation demonstrated by Jesus. We should speak out for the marginalized, those left behind and forgotten. Many of us are just too busy judging the world to be a part of saving it. It is easy to judge from the dugout—to sit passively in condemnation of others. As we are out of the game, our local community and the world look on, waiting for our stand, hoping for some caring and responding. Oh my, how we fail here.

Don't be despondent. Inactivity is easy to fix. Become involved by following the example of those with caring and responding hearts. If you don't immediately see needs, ask and look until you find them. Get out of that dugout and start warming up. Remember whom you are playing for, the One with all the authority, the Creator of this and every other world. He wants us in the game.

CHAPTER 4

What Causes Mean Christianity?

There is no place for Christian meanness, not in the lives of individual Christians nor in the corporate body of Christ. In this book's introduction, I wrote that meanness is antithetical to Christianity. Antithetical concepts are polar opposites. Meanness, then, is the antithesis of Christ and the one thing that should not be associated with the Christian faith.

Emulating Jesus and being mean are simply incompatible. Like on the neighborhood baseball diamond, you have to pick a side—to be either inclusive, kind, and loving all the time or not to be like Christ. Mean Christians are not living like Jesus, and their efforts for the faith are ineffective, if not unattractive.

The mean person who claims Christianity looks like everyone else. If anything, the hypocrisy of colliding values makes mean Christians appear worse than others. Think about it: Why would a seeker of truth consider Jesus if His followers are indistinguishable from the worst of those who do not know Him?

Unchecked meanness in Christians draws the public eye. Stories about mean Christians become big news, affecting not only those involved but the overall brand of Christianity itself. One broadly reported display of Christian meanness too often counteracts the countless Christlike actions of the Elaines and Jacks of this world.

What, then, is the body of Christ to do? We must first understand meanness and its myriad causes. As a professor, I'm interested in cause. For example, I've studied what causes speech and language disorders. What I've learned has made me a better clinician and teacher. When cause is understood, change is possible.

Knowing the causes of mean Christianity can help Christians distance themselves from meanness, if not eliminate it entirely. To make a baseball analogy, the reliable but slumping hitter has to analyze his swing—to break down his actions in a manner that allows for correction. So it is with Christian meanness. We as individual Christians and the corporate body of Christ must take a careful look at the individual and collective roots of Christian meanness.

Before considering the causes of Christian meanness, let's clarify two points. First, all of us get angry. Momentary bouts with anger are human and often occur as a result of understandable frustrations. While Christians should work to minimize anger in their lives, I'm not referring to fleeting anger in the following discussion of meanness. Second, I think meanness has common origins whether expressed by Christians or non-Christians. Mean is mean. The problem is this: We shouldn't see meanness in the lives of professing Christians.

So what causes meanness? Six things come to mind: personal history, lack of knowledge, fear, obsession with self, judgment, and hatred. We will consider each separately, but it is important to note that these causes interact. For example, one's personal history can contribute to stereotypic assumptions, fear, and judgment.

PERSONAL HISTORY

In Chapter 1, I shared some of my own personal history and noted that I experienced considerable privilege and had the good fortune to observe many more positive than negative formative models. Over time, I've learned that my experience is atypical.

In the United States, sixty percent of adults report being abused during childhood.[1] One in four children have encountered a traumatic event

---

1. Mental Health Connection of Tarrant County, "Statistics," Recognize Trauma: Change a Child's Future, http://www.recognizetrauma.org/statistics.php. [March 30, 2017]

by age four, and almost forty percent have witnessed a violent act.[2] These statistics are stunning, yet there is more to personal history than violence and abuse. For many, life has been loveless. Parents, siblings, and others may have offered little in the way of affection, praise, or encouragement. As a result, for some people successful relationships are challenging if not impossible. Misfortune, loss, and failure have colored the lives of others, contributing to discouragement and joylessness.

Personal histories can offer less obvious negative influences as well. For many people, important figures in their lives have modeled habits and values that led them to make poor life choices. Substance abuse comes to mind, but one could also argue that formative experiences focusing on the single-minded pursuit of wealth or achievement can also be destructive.

Are Christians impervious to negative personal histories? There is no reason to assume so. We can tell ourselves that Christian life examples reduce these influences, but is that true? Remember, all have sinned and fall short of the glory of God (Rom 3:23). We are all sinners, and even Christian models are less than perfect.

I'll take the notion of imperfect Christian life figures one uncomfortable step further. Meanness is often modeled as righteous indignation by Christian leaders, individual Christians, and the corporate body of Christ. Anyone told (directly or indirectly) to disregard or dislike others who don't look, live, love, or worship like them is being immersed in meanness. Meanness is too often disguised as aspirational religious dogma.

I have personally experienced mean faith-based dogma. Though my early church experiences surrounded me largely with moderate influences, I was taught to be skeptical, if not dismissive, of Christian faiths that differed too dramatically from my own. I remember church teachings that portrayed the practices and beliefs of specific Christian denominations as wrong. This clearly influenced my perceptions of many individuals I met later in life. Interestingly, the more time I spent with people of varied faith backgrounds, the more I observed faith-based commonalities rather than differences.

How does personal history lead to meanness? Do you see your mother or father in your actions, in how you stand or offer a greeting, in the things you say and do? Every day, I see and hear my father's voice in my own. Thank goodness his model was positive. There is no getting around the fact that our lives reflect what we experience.

2. Ibid.

If, then, we experience meanness, we may be more likely to offer it. The child who hears hateful talk or experiences violence may gravitate to unkindness or perpetrate hostility. Likewise, the individual who has lived without love and affection may well struggle with emotions and default to indifference, if not meanness. Similarly, those who have failed repeatedly or experienced misfortune or loss may be understandably bitter toward others.

Several aspects of personal history mentioned above may be beyond one's control. We don't get to choose our early role models or life experiences. Mean religious dogma, however, is different. People offering meanness from positions of religious authority are exploiting an innocent captive audience. I'm continually drawn to the millstone reference in Jesus' teaching (Matt 18:6; Mark 9:42; Luke 17:2). Leading individuals away from the teachings of Jesus, in my opinion, sets you up for a millstone necklace and a deep swim. Let me be more direct: Instructional faith-based rhetoric that does not reflect the themes of Christ described in Chapter 2 is, in baseball terms, way off base.

What can be done about personal history as a root of Christian meanness? Thank goodness for forgiveness and grace. These concepts are explored in chapters to follow, but for now let's just say that Christians get re-dos or opportunities for a fresh start. You may be saying "Everyone gets re-dos." My response is "Yes . . . but." The "but" here relates to what happens when one genuinely experiences God's grace.

A dear friend of mine recently told me, "Bill, life is about choices." He is so right! Each day we make choices. We choose to continue life courses or to change them. Truly understanding the power of choice is an invaluable personal epiphany. So often, people feel caught in negative personal histories that are spiraling out of control and bound to repeat what they've lived or learned.

But we do have choices. Change is possible, though its costs may be considerable. Implementing a choice that changes one's life direction may be the start of a difficult journey, but, thank God, there are resources to help, such as professional and faith-based counseling. When traveling a difficult life path of change, you're not alone. Remember the road to Emmaus (Luke 24:13–24)—Jesus is always up for a walk. He is a pretty capable exercise partner too. Think of those Chris Tomlin lyrics from *Whom Shall I Fear*: "The One who goes before me, the One who stands behind. The God of angel armies, He is a friend of mine."

LACK OF KNOWLEDGE

Meanness can be the result of a lack of knowledge. This often goes hand-in-hand with fear—the next cause on my list. For now, let's consider the impact of what we don't know on the origin of meanness.

The world has changed dramatically over the past one hundred years. A century ago, few people left their communities. It was atypical, if not unheard of, to encounter difference as it is defined today—differences in ethnicity, religion, race, or sexual orientation. The lack of mobility created homogeneity with respect to appearance, culture, ideas, and language.

Societal immobility can be beautiful. I live in the gorgeous mountains of western North Carolina, and the cultural wealth of mountain communities is evident. The lack of population mobility, however, has its challenges. For example, if our experiences are largely common, it becomes easy to draw "us" and "them" conclusions when encountering difference. From there, we are one small step from embracing stereotypes that minimize individual variance in others and contribute to fear and meanness in those who hold them.

Immobility is more than population stagnation. When we become certain of our opinions and positions, we fail to be intellectually mobile—to consider views or perspectives that collide with our own. Intellectual immobility creates rigid worldviews that, again, lead to stereotype, fear, and meanness. As we adopt and adhere to strict worldviews, we look past individuality and default to collective assumptions, drawing conclusions based upon judgments that often have little merit.

If, for example, I hold an immobile worldview that all Muslims hate Christians, then I see every Muslim as a threat, set on harming me or unwilling to peacefully coexist. Let's assume I believed this during my graduate-school years. I would have avoided sharing a house with my friend Ghazi and, in turn, missed out on a meaningful friendship. If I held this view today, I would have declined a recent invitation to be a part of an emerging interfaith group in my community. I would have lost the opportunity to meet several lovely people from a variety of faith and cultural backgrounds.

To avoid immobility, we must step out of our comfort zones. If our lives are predictable and our communities are closed, we must seek out opportunities to encounter diversity. I'll take this a step further. We should push ourselves intellectually by studying those who differ from us, taking a careful and factual assessment of difference whether it applies to race, ethnicity, culture, faith, or sexual orientation. I hear a few readers rumbling, "The Bible is enough for me." Yes, the Bible is a great place to start, especially if you focus on the words and actions of Jesus.

You may attribute my advice to a "liberal," academic perspective. To the contrary, I think all people, liberal or conservative, should challenge their assumptions—their physical and intellectual immobility. Recently, a liberal friend at church shared her confusion and hopelessness after the 2016 election. To my great surprise, she said she had embarked on a personal journey to understand people who did not share her opinion. This involved physically entering the worlds of others and honestly talking with them about their beliefs and aspirations. Now that is mobility.

What if an arrogant baseball team decided they never needed to play teams from outside their region? They were so good, in fact, that they did not need to study their opponents either. Such a team would be destined to fail. Not playing a range of teams or knowing their opponents' strengths and weaknesses would certainly reduce the likelihood of winning. Mobility and preparedness seem reasonable if not prudent when offered as advice to our imaginary team, yet applying these concepts to our life can be threatening. Comfort zones are called that for a reason—they *are* comfortable.

In sum, not knowing is a condition we should all avoid. In John 8:32 Jesus says, "Then you will know the truth, and the truth will set you free." Meanness that emerges from ignorance is avoidable. This requires a little boldness and curiosity on our part, but the effort can be very rewarding.

FEAR

Fear is a common human emotion. What do you fear—illness, loss of control, personal tragedy? If I let it, my mind defaults to fear so quickly. As suggested above, fear as a cause of meanness goes hand-in-hand with ignorance. If something is unknown, it is easy to fear.

I've feared many unknowns. In my early forties, I received unusual medical results during what I had assumed would be routine prostate screenings. Although my test findings had several possible explanations, I immediately feared the worst. When my children were small, I feared everything on their behalf—falls, fevers, hurt feelings. As they began to drive, my mind went to awful places each time they pulled out of the driveway. As I draw nearer to retirement, I fear whether I will have sufficient financial resources over my lifetime. Fear is both a reality and a burden.

Fear typically leads in one of two directions. It either locks us down physically, intellectually, and emotionally, or it challenges us to act positively. When locked down, we default to avoidance or confrontation. Confrontation often leads to meanness.

Let's say someone has never encountered a person who is transgender. What they "know" about transgender individuals has come from media related to legislative efforts to restrict bathroom usage based on birth gender (remember I live in North Carolina). The rhetoric they have encountered has suggested that transgender people are predators, especially of children. When this person meets a transgender person face-to-face, there is certainly the possibility of avoidance based on fear. There is also the possibility of confrontation and meanness. In this example, meanness may be a passive "those people" reaction, or it may be quite active, expressed in a hurtful comment or an exclusionary action.

If we take the same example but follow a different reactive path, fear is not so troubling. For example, say the uninformed individual described above initially experiences fear about transgender people. He, however, chooses intellectual mobility—to explore what is known about the likelihood that being transgender relates to increased predatory behavior. His study leads him to believe that the information supporting restrictive legislation is not factual. When this individual later meets a transgender person, he is at least less likely to be confrontational. There is even the possibility that information can facilitate a positive exchange in a face-to-face encounter.

I know what it's like to be locked down by fear. As a fairly young man I heard and largely accepted homophobic perspectives from some people around me. What I heard contributed to avoidance on my part, both of the topic and of individuals whom I assumed might be gay or lesbian. Increasingly, I came to know and care deeply for people who were open homosexuals. I dealt with my fear by unlearning what was taught to me and re-learning through positive life experiences.

Our fear of other differences—such as in race, nationality, gender, ethnicity, and religion—can also potentially lead to meanness. Regardless of the source of fear, our potential reactions remain the same: we can become locked down, or we can choose a more positive and potentially cathartic, life-changing path.

Have you ever wondered how Jesus would respond to things that make us fearful? We know He admonishes us not to worry (Matt 6:25–27).

We also know He faced down the biggest fear of all, death (Luke 22:42). How would He face fears associated with difference, be it color, ethnicity, nationality, alternative faiths, gender, or sexuality? We get some idea in His response to the woman at the well (John 4:7–15), His ministry to the centurion (Luke 7:6–10), His parable of the Good Samaritan (Luke 10:30–37). He wouldn't lock down. He would care and respond. He expects the same of you and me.

OBSESSION WITH SELF

What does self-centeredness have to do with meanness? When we supremely value ourselves, our decisions reflect selfish priorities. Sadly, selfishness comes with rewards. Vigorously pursuing our interests at the cost of others often yields tangible benefits—we're recognized, promoted, and attain more. Admittedly, this is success according to the world. Is it, however, success as defined by the life of Christ? Though self-centeredness can lead to worldly achievement, it creates a dangerous vortex of inwardly focused life choices.

I am far too self-centered. Too much of what I earn goes to my wants and desires. When your hobbies include stringed instruments, this can get pricey. I also protect time to address my interests—the needs of others have to wait. I have to admit, my attention is disproportionately on me, even as I try to live more intentionally.

Let's consider the relationship between self-centeredness and meanness. If one becomes singularly focused on self, others are perceived at best as an annoyance and at worst as competition for time and resources. If "other" opportunities arise (described earlier as path chances), the self-absorbed person can easily default to meanness. After all, others are obstacles to self-pursuits. Selfish Christians fit nicely into the compartmentalized expression of faith I've discussed several times in this book. As Christians separate faith from other aspects of life, there is more time for attention on self.

It may take a very self-absorbed Christian to demonstrate much of the meanness discussed in Chapter 3. It may be more likely for selfish Christians to appear uninterested in or unaffected by the needs of others, but remember that disinterest can also be viewed as meanness.

JUDGMENT

Why do we judge? I can think of two reasons: We think we're right, and we're arrogant. Sometimes we are so certain we're right, we can't hold back our opinions. You've heard of moral high ground? We claim the moral high ground when we judge because we are convinced we're right—we know it, and we know God does too! (Of course, I'm not saying Christians are always right—far from it!) Claiming the moral high ground can light a fire that leads to righteous indignation. The more certain we are that we are indeed right, the more we are prepared to dig in and go to the mat with those who disagree with us.

This book has addressed several tender issues, and here I introduce another—abortion. I totally understand righteous indignation over abortion. I believe, however, that a stance against abortion is on shaky ground if it is not accompanied by opposition to the death penalty, to needless and inhumane slaughter of animals, and to the thoughtless destruction of our planet. Failure to view life with reverence in all its forms creates a moral inconsistency. Finally, those against abortion should also support nutritional, educational, and health programs for children and families. Abortion, like so many other issues, is very complex.

I'm not writing to argue for or against contentious subjects; I'm simply questioning how we respond to those who hold positions that differ from our own, whether it's abortion, faith, race, sexual orientation, or something else. When we dig our heels in to judge, how do we treat others? Are our words and actions mean? Being indignant pushes us into a territory where emotions rule, and, often, we regret our behaviors.

How does arrogance relate to judgment? Arrogance shares a kinship with the moral high ground, yet is distinctly different. An arrogant person holds an air of self-importance. An arrogant person chooses not to attempt to relate to the perspectives or plights of others because "others" just aren't worth it. Often arrogant people have little understanding of the trials and challenges of those they judge. In fact, arrogance may well surface because one has enjoyed privilege.

Being "right" and arrogance can certainly lead to judgment, which, in turn, is a slippery slope to meanness. According to Matt 7:1, "Do not judge or you too will be judged." I think we're best to keep our distance on this one. Well, you may ask, if we can't judge, who can? Remember the baseball analogy? God is behind the plate. Let's leave judgment to the only One who can do it perfectly. A little less time judging would give us all more time for caring and responding.

HATRED

Hatred as a source of meanness—that's a no brainer, right? Of course hatred leads to meanness. We can easily point to historical times when hatred motivated people to perpetrate and accept meanness. In the past hundred years, possibly no example of hatred is clearer than the rise of anti-Semitism in Nazi Germany. Hitler blamed the Jews for Germany's problems—the loss of World War I and the nation's subsequent economic calamity. German leadership identified the Jews as a scapegoat for Germany's failures, leading to the arrest, isolation, and death of millions. Good people were duped here—the German populous became caught up in hatred. It was unifying and attractive.

Today, groups share their disdain for others publicly, in person, in print, and online. Hatred continues to unify people with respect to issues of the day such as immigration, race, gender equality, religion, and sexual orientation. Hatred also surfaces in more acceptable ways, such as in strong feelings against those who hold worldviews that differ from our own. As hatred gains traction, people feel empowered to speak and act meanly.

What are the origins of hatred? We can start with two of our sources of meanness—personal history and lack of knowledge. People who hate have often learned or experienced hatred from individuals they value and respect—from their parents, their community, and, yes, their church. Others have turned to hatred because they lack an understanding of the issues at hand. For them, it is safer to default to hatred than to explore issues with intellectual flexibility.

Hatred also surfaces when people are frustrated, when they haven't enjoyed the success they had hoped for, or when they see that success in others whom they feel are less deserving. Finally, hatred can evolve from righteous indignation. Remember my comparison of righteous indignation and walking on a rotting bridge in Chapter 3? On that bridge, each step is fraught with risks, as boards pop and crack, and one wrong step results in disaster. Pursuing what is intended as righteous indignation to illogical and extreme ends can be both hateful and disastrous. The bombing of abortion clinics is a good example of indignation gone awry.

I've seen hatred on the baseball diamond. When two teams that truly hate each other play, bad things happen. Good hitters strike out; good fielders make errors; fights emerge. Losing control in an athletic competition doesn't typically work out well.

Hatred is a consuming and harmful source of meanness in today's world, one that, if unchecked, leads down life paths that in no way resemble the life of Christ. Although deeply rooted, is hatred an unsolvable problem?

By no means. Remember the first theme of Christ's likeness presented in Chapter 2—His authority? When things seem unsolvable, Jesus has the answer and has your back. The Guy who calms storms can change your heart and the hearts of those who perpetrate hatred against you.

In baseball terms, hatred makes us feel like we're trailing in the late innings. But the game isn't over. You can't see it, but I'm smiling now because the home team bats last. We get the final swings at the plate. How each of us reacts to hatred will go a long way toward extending or ending it. You're on deck. What will you do?

Thus far, I have considered several individual causes of meanness and suggested that meanness results when these causes interact. Now it is time to take a larger view of cause. When watching a nationally televised baseball game, the cameras occasionally zoom out to provide a sweeping view of the entire field of play. Sometimes, for particularly important games, the broadest view can come from a blimp circling the stadium.

Broad views can be helpful because we see the big picture as it relates to problems and solutions. If we take a very broad view of meanness in the lives of individual Christians and the corporate body of Christ, what do we see? I see people who aren't living like Jesus. If the Christian life can be defined by the primacy of Christ in our lives and by our efforts to emulate Him, then I see either people who are failing to be Christlike or some who have never experienced the life-changing, cathartic possibilities that come with complete submission to His authority.

I get failing. I fail all the time. If meanness is a byproduct of periodic spiritual derailment, we can respond with a genuine effort to walk intentionally with Christ—minute to minute, hour to hour, day to day. You'll remember that my efforts to walk more intentionally resulted from a worshipful week in which I encountered God at every turn. From that point, my predictable expression of faith (church attendance) was insufficient. I believe periodic meanness can be addressed by the active, intentional pursuit of Christ's likeness. As we work to play our position for Him, there will be little time or motivation for meanness.

What if meanness comes from a different place? What if some who profess Christ have never met Him in a life-changing way? All the time, I see people who claim to be Christians yet appear unchanged by Him. It makes me wonder what or whom they are following. If you've met Jesus personally, as Paul did on the road to Damascus (Luke 24:13–35), your life changes. There is no other option. The things that were once important lose their appeal. You realize that your efforts fail without Him. You are drawn into a relationship that is life-altering, a journey that, as long as you are all in, only moves forward—sometimes at a faster rate than others.

It's like the ballplayer who can't make the big leagues on his own. All his personal efforts to improve are ultimately disappointing. He eventually recognizes that the improvement he seeks requires more, and he signs with a personal trainer. The trainer knows his business. In fact, the trainer may have been a successful player in the past—he has credibility and authority. The ballplayer commits every waking moment to following the guidance of the trainer. Over time, change happens—the snap of the pitch is sharper, the swing is more efficient. The player's hard work makes a difference, but only when it occurs within a relationship in which a mentor guides his efforts.

In the example above, the trainer does what he does for financial reward and the likelihood of additional player referrals. When we accept Christ, Jesus does what He does because He loves us and seeks our fellowship. All we have to do is recognize our inability to live this life alone and His ultimate authority over us as God. His gift of newness and grace then begins to change us in every way.

I'm reminded of the old hymn "Have Thine Own Way." The lyrics tell the story of the cathartic nature of knowing Jesus.

> Have thine own way, Lord,
> Have Thine own way;
> Thou art the Potter,
> I am the clay.
> Mold me and make me
> After Thy will,
> While I am waiting,
> Yielded and still.

As Christians, we are the clay, the substance to be molded after His will, His likeness. People claiming to be Christians but mired in constant meanness must prayerfully question their relationship with Christ. If they have yet to meet Him in a life-changing way, that possibility is a simple invitation away. I promise you a relationship with Jesus will change your life.

For some, it may be time to stop trying to play the game without His mentorship. How this world could change if everyone who claimed Christ played his or her position all day, every day.

CHAPTER 5

What Are the Costs of Mean Christianity?

Costs are what we offer or give up in pursuit of something. There are obvious monetary costs associated with everyday life—food, shelter, and clothing, among others. There are also costs tied to common daily actions. The cost of my decision to wear a favorite shirt, for example, may be time at the ironing board. The cost of two sodas in the morning (I like my caffeine cold) may be an early stop at the restroom (remember I'm sixty years old). In both of these examples, I give up time. I weigh my options and make a choice.

Costs are a part of life and the choices we make. Sometimes life choices result in severe costs. The decision to be unfaithful may compromise a marriage and destroy a family. Drinking and driving may end a life. When choices result in the loss of love or life, costs are particularly heavy.

Before this book, I had not considered the potential costs associated with a conscious decision to be mean. This thought raises several questions. Does meanness cost those who offer it, or only their victims? Does meanness exhibited by individual Christians and the corporate body of Christ cost the faith? Finally, can the costs of meanness motivate mean Christians to change?

Difficult change doesn't occur without strong motivation. Think of the talented but lazy baseball player who goes through the motions on the field. While his abilities may initially keep him in the game, poor practice habits will eventually cost him his role as a starter. Once on the sidelines, he can continue his ineffective approach to the game, or he can use his benching as motivation to change as a player.

In this chapter, I argue that the costs of Christian meanness should motivate change. The idea that some Christians don't see meanness in themselves continues to trouble me. Remember my adage that you can't hit what you can't see. Hopefully, Chapters 3 and 4 have brought home that Christian meanness is real. However, if some Christians question whether change is needed, we must explore the costs of meanness—to ourselves, to others, and to the Christian faith.

HOW DOES MEANNESS COST THE INDIVIDUAL MEAN CHRISTIAN OR THE MEAN CORPORATE BODY OF CHRIST?

To consider cost, it is helpful to revisit my definition of Christian meanness. In Chapter 3, I propose that a mean Christian claims Christ yet at least some of the time treats others in petty, offensive, or despicable ways. I also note that selfishness can motivate mean Christianity. What costs are associated with these behaviors?

Pettiness can be defined as a preoccupation with trivial matters, a small-mindedness that leads to spite. I've been there; I can easily default to pettiness, especially when I feel I've been wronged. Can churches be petty too? Sure they can. One of the most divisive elements in the early church was petty legalism (throughout the book of Acts). Many believers were preoccupied with the role of Jewish traditions and practices in their new faith (Acts 10:9–16).

What does being petty cost us as individuals or as a corporate body? It takes our eyes off the ball. Think of the baseball hitter or fielder. If these players aren't looking at the baseball, they have no hope of executing their jobs on the field. Oh sure, I remember a couple of little league games when I closed my eyes and stabbed successfully at the ball with my bat or glove. As a rule, though, ballplayers, as well as Christians, need to keep their eyes open.

If we are too preoccupied with the trivial (the sins of our neighbors, the faults of our brothers and sisters in Christ) we don't see needs all around us. We fall off the paths of others. Interestingly, Jesus saw the sins of those He met, but only long enough to forgive, care, and respond. Stories of the woman at the well (John 4:7–15) or the woman caught in the act of adultery (John 8:3–11) come to mind.

Pettiness can also lead to score-keeping and spite. It is simply human nature to keep tallies of perceived wrongs. As the scorecard grows, spite builds. Soon we focus on getting even. Petty score-keeping, like a misguided preoccupation with the trivial, takes our eyes off Christ and His kingdom.

So, what does pettiness cost Christians? What are we choosing to give up? First and foremost, the inward focus that accompanies pettiness makes it difficult to recognize Jesus' authority. The deep and abiding reverence and the cathartic possibilities that come with recognizing and honoring Jesus' authority can't happen unless we're "all in" with respect to our relationship with Him. When we're petty, we're not all in. Second, pettiness takes us out of the game; it keeps us from seeing the needs of others, from caring and responding. Third, if focused on the trivial, we are less likely to be authentic, and our bar for life is anything but aspirational. Finally, pettiness is an obstacle to obeying Jesus' command to "follow Me." In sum, pettiness costs Christians opportunities to be Christlike.

What about offensiveness or despicability? We're wading in the deep waters of cost here. When the individual Christian or corporate body of Christ is truly offensive or despicable, they have wandered far off base. Have you ever seen a good baseball rundown where a base runner is caught between the bases after taking too big a lead or attempting to steal? The runner runs back and forth as the fielders throw the ball, coming ever closer each time to tagging him out. Almost always, the runner is tagged.

If, as individual Christians or churches, we are offensive or despicable, we're caught in a rundown. Our behaviors are so inconsistent with the central message of Christ that we find ourselves uncomfortably in no man's land—outside of the Christian faith as it was intended.

When you know Christ and have enjoyed His forgiveness and grace, there is not much worse than knowing that your behaviors don't reflect His values and His love. This is one cost of being offensive or despicable. Another is joy. Simply put, these behaviors make our lives darker. When we're offensive or despicable, our focus narrows, meanness builds, and we lose sight of the joys of living.

I'd like to think that I've avoided this side of meanness, but I'm not sure. There certainly have been times when anger ruled my day. Whether I translated this into offensive or despicable behavior is debatable, but the darkness I experienced is not. We can all agree that offensive and despicable meanness robs us of simple joy. The loss of joy is a cost of being mean.

As with pettiness, offensiveness and despicability also cost Christians because they steer us far from Christ's likeness. In fact, these behaviors are totally inconsistent with my themes presented in Chapter 2. If our goal is to emulate Jesus, Christians can't be offensive or despicable.

Finally, what about the costs of selfishness? This hits close to home. I kid with friends that, unlike others, I only began to lose my egocentrism a couple of years ago. While I'm trying to be funny, my comment is sadly truthful. Too much of my life has been about my interests and my wants.

In Chapter 3, I tied selfishness to meanness because it makes us too inwardly focused. Our obsession with self blinds us to the needs of others. I suggested that knowing Christ is reorienting. It puts God first, others second, and us last. When selfishness alters that order, we miss so much. Selfishness costs us in that we lose out on a life-changing relationship with our Creator. Our narrow focus also keeps us from knowing, serving, and loving others.

Let's consider a broader view of the cost of meanness to perpetrators. Remember that I've suggested that mean is mean whether someone is a Christian or not. I do, however, believe that the individual Christian or corporate body of Christ exhibiting meanness experiences one cost that a non-Christian does not.

Think about it. Christians who make an intentional effort to follow Jesus, to be like Him, live life differently. They are caring and responding with authenticity; living their values of selflessness, humility, love, compassion, kindness, and faith; holding a high bar for life that encourages their best while keeping them humble; and playing their position. Being Christlike makes Christians other-centered and leads to a keen awareness of people in their path. This kind of life puts Christians "in the zone" with respect to personal relationships and the needs of those around them.

Have you heard of being in the zone? A hitter in the zone knows the location of the next pitch before it leaves the pitcher's hand. A pitcher is in the zone when every throw trims the plate, leaving batters baffled. I think that meanness keeps Christians from ever getting in the "Christlike" zone. Meanness is like the gnats at home plate that swarm around the batter's head. It keeps us from seeing others and from entering a perfect zone of service and love.

WHAT DOES MEANNESS COST ITS VICTIMS?

My bet is that we've all been on the receiving end of meanness. I remember being a pigeon-toed elementary-aged child. It was very noticeable—still is if you look! When I walked or ran, my feet turned in badly. My parents believed in medical specialists, like the "pigeon-toed expert" who practiced in Jackson, Mississippi. My father and mother took me to Dr. Blake at least once a year. He was a nice man, but his remedy for me was embarrassing. Dr. Blake had my folks order black dress shoes with soles adjusted to turn my feet outward. I guess my mother and father never realized how this made me look as a grade-schooler. Every day, I'd enter class with my very ugly shoes. I might as well have had a bullseye on my back. Kids were mean. Needless to say, I rejected the shoes quickly in favor of just being pigeon-toed.

Not only have we experienced meanness, we've observed it too—bullying, unkindness in attempted humor, exclusion, violence in actions and speech, and so on. This list is certainly not exhaustive. When you think about how meanness affects those receiving it, several things come to mind—embarrassment, hurt feelings, lower self-esteem, loneliness, physical harm. In aggregate, where can these effects lead?

Most of us shake off the occasional meanness we experience. When we can't, it might darken our mood or, on bad days, push us to retaliation. Where, though, does meanness lead people who receive it constantly? Unless their spirit is unusually strong, it can be crushing. Meanness, inflicted consistently, wears down their personhood, alters their aspirations, and limits their life potential.

As a speech-language pathologist, I hear about meanness experienced by those with communication disorders. Face it, if you can't communicate effectively, you can become the target of ridicule. A dear friend who stutters has shared a bit about the meanness he experienced as a child. Due to his inability to speak fluently, he was teased and even placed in educational settings for children with more substantial disabilities. Luckily, my friend rose above these circumstances to become a successful therapist and university educator who now helps others who stutter. I'm afraid his ultimately positive experience, however, is atypical.

There are many stories today about the costs of persistent meanness—children who commit suicide or perpetrate unimaginable violence after being ridiculed or teased, or adults who attribute criminal behaviors to meanness and violence in their early lives. Clearly, the aggregate victim-related costs of meanness are potentially quite high.

As I write about victims of meanness, I'm struck by how life experiences differ for each of us. Those fortunate enough to have lived in loving homes with caring life models definitely have advantages. Children often grow into adults who largely imitate what they've experienced, though I know this is not entirely true. Life cycles can be broken.

We must remember that meanness, as well as kindness, can be "handed down." Therefore, an unanticipated effect of meanness to those who experience it can be a reciprocal mean response contributing to a cycle of meanness. That is, the victim of meanness may themselves become mean, propagating the behavior into the future.

The phenomenon described above sounds a little like a bad zombie movie, in which people get infected and then infect others. This amusing analogy is anything but funny when applied to Christian meanness. We simply don't need more mean people in this world, much less mean Christians!

WHAT DOES MEANNESS COST THE CHRISTIAN FAITH?

I'm using the phrase "Christian faith" to describe the corporate Christian church (comprised of its believers) and its brand and actions. I could sum this up with the phrase "the cause of Christ." Here, we're considering the very big picture of Christianity.

Meanness, even in its mildest forms, creates a perception problem. I shared in Chapter 3 that branding is critical. Products, organizations, and services all live or die based upon their brand. Recently, Volkswagen and General Motors have taken brand hits caused by discoveries regarding false vehicle emission claims. At least in Volkswagen's case, fines were paid and vehicle owners were compensated in an attempt to salvage the company's reputation.

I have shared that the Christian brand is damaged each time an episode of Christian meanness surfaces. Maybe we shouldn't worry. After all, who is paying attention? Everyone! We live in a time in which it is often vogue to claim Christianity. I'm not saying to actually be a Christian, mind you, just to *claim* to be. People wear crosses, hold hands as they pray in restaurants, offer God's blessing in passing, and put the Ichthys symbol (the fish) on their businesses and vehicles. Again, these actions aren't wrong, and I understand the rationale—not being ashamed of who you are and wanting others to associate you with Christ. There is just one problem: People are watching.

My church recently took part in a county initiative to "Be the Church" in the broader community. Congregations received bright red t-shirts with the slogan proudly and prominently displayed. A good idea right? It is, but only if we're living like Jesus. After the effort was well under way, I encountered someone wearing the red t-shirt screaming and cursing in a local store. It was an ugly scene and a brand killer.

The costs of negative perceptions on the Christian faith are pervasive—reduced appeal, limited credibility, negative stereotypes, hypocrisy, and the list goes on. Perception matters, especially in an image-conscious world.

Meanness costs the faith in other ways. One akin to perception is message clarity. As a professor, I like it when a theory is simple and elegant, when all aspects point to a reasoned conclusion. The physical life of Christ created few "message" problems for His followers. His words and actions were clear and consistent, and, as this book argues, as Christians we should consistently emulate His life and His message.

If factions of the faith exhibit meanness, how does the broader Christian message appear? Inconsistent? Less credible? Mahatma Gandhi was reported to have said, "I like your Christ, I do not like your Christians. Your Christians are so unlike your Christ." Though some have doubted the authenticity of this quote, it certainly highlights inconsistencies in the lives of Christians. I understand that the Christian life is a journey—that Christ's complete likeness is unattainable for us humans. That said, should we not work for message clarity and consistency, especially when it comes to eradicating meanness? Think about it. If we could take meanness, in all the forms described in this book, off the table for those critiquing Christianity, how would the faith appear?

Finally, meanness costs the faith followers. A damaged brand and inconsistent message caused by mean Christians make Christianity anything but appealing. Meanness turns away countless seekers who might otherwise find the message of Christ attractive, even life-changing.

In my sixty years, I've encountered myriad people seeking God but afraid or unwilling to consider Christianity. I've met even more who have had some "Christian experiences" but drifted away over time. They have either been hurt by Christians or the church, become indifferent to the faith, or found comfort in a compartmentalized expression of Christianity requiring few commitments or sacrifices. Many are looking for reasons not to explore the faith further or to truly engage. Unfortunately, we as professing Christians readily assist them. We fail to live in ways that suggest that Jesus matters. Meanness has been at the center of our failure.

Many of the seekers described above are desperate for meaning in their lives. If you've had a cathartic experience with Christ, you have to want that for others. It is the perfect solution for our world today.

What if all Christians lived like Jesus? What if every single person who claimed Christ emulated His values alone? Obviously, meanness is off the table then, right? Can you imagine the headlines in newspapers—the unexplained kindness offered to others, the unconditional love, the selflessness? What would happen to the Christian brand—the clarity and consistency of the faith and its message? Do you think this might spark some interest in Christianity?

Let me conclude this discussion by saying I'm not necessarily recruiting here. I believe that you don't have to recruit when what you offer is genuine and authentic. Quality messages, like very good teams, attract followers.

If we all played our positions, oh what possibilities would abound! The world would change. The faith would be attractive to others. It can happen. It will, however, require change.

BENEFITS OF MEANNESS?

I've spent considerable effort discussing the costs of meanness. The fact that we see it in the lives of Christians and others suggests that there are also benefits to being mean. If I am asking Christians to change their behavior with respect to meanness, it is only fair that I acknowledge and discuss the benefits of being mean. Again, change is hard, and all of us need to be convinced that it's worth the effort.

What are the benefits of meanness? After some careful thought, two come to mind. First, let's reflect on the emotional rush and the sense of power that people experience when they are mean. Undeniably, being mean gives you a rush, especially if you feel you are in the right. There have been more than a few times in my life when I felt hurt by another person and acted in a mean way in turn. I have to say there was a momentary rush of emotion. I had righted a wrong in my opinion, and the recipient of my meanness deserved my retaliation.

The problem with momentary rushes is that they are just that—momentary. In fact, most of the time when I've acted this way, my actions simply perpetuated a cycle of meanness. Someone offended me, then I offended them; off we went, cycling out of control. Although I enjoyed a brief rush when it was my turn, it quickly left when I was offended again.

So we get a rush, but even that often costs us as yet another distraction. When we are drawn into a "tit-for-tat," we veer off the path of others. We lose the opportunity to care and respond. This type of distraction takes us off another path as well. Remember, becoming Christlike is a journey, and the more we participate in behaviors inconsistent with His likeness, the further we drift away from Christ and our efforts to emulate Him.

What about power as a benefit? The rush mentioned above can be associated with perceived or actual power. When we perpetrate meanness, we often feel powerful. After all, our actions have diminished the standing of someone else. We win, right? Or do we? I get that we might feel superior and even powerful, but do we win?

I remember a story in which darkness seemed to win. There was this Guy who lived a sinless life. He cared for and responded to others with love and humility. In spite of all the good He did, His life threatened authorities to the point that they exerted their power to stop Him. They killed Him. Jesus was on the receiving end of ultimate meanness when He was tried, crucified, and killed. Did meanness win? Thank God, it did not!

Power gained through meanness is fleeting at best. It is also inconsistent with the themes of Christ presented in Chapter 2. Many in Jesus' day expected the Messiah to embody power as defined by the world and overthrow the harsh rule of the Romans. Jesus ushered in a new order all right. He did not do so, however, through conventional political or military power. Maybe power, as the world defines it, is not so attractive.

CAN THE COST OF MEANNESS MOTIVATE MEAN CHRISTIANS TO CHANGE?

This is an interesting question. In my heart, I believe the answer is "yes." In the process of writing this book, I've come to realize that there are multiple factions within the larger body of Christ. You have the "all in" folks. Meanness, with this group, is fleeting if it occurs at all. You also have the striving group. I put myself in this category. I want to be all in, but I get in my own way. I guess strivers can be characterized as works in progress. Meanness may come a little more easily to those of us who are striving. Then, you have the compartmentalized. I've spoken at length about this group. They are the Christians who keep life neatly and separately ordered. For them, faith is one compartment of several that really don't overlap and that are pursued separately. I think meanness, especially as it relates to selfishness, may be a more frequent problem with this group. I also think the compartmentalized can drift into more egregious forms of meanness because their faith is isolated and not interacting with their daily lives. Finally, you have claimers. This group claims Christ but just doesn't seem to get Christianity as I define it in Chapter 2. Claimers are at serious risk of some of the more extreme forms of meanness. Incredibly, they may perpetrate meanness and justify it by righteous indignation.

If you are not all in as a Christian all of the time, you are susceptible to meanness. Too many of us aren't all in. We're lukewarm. Do you remember the Biblical admonition about being lukewarm? Rev 3:16 says, "because you are lukewarm—neither hot nor cold—I am about to spit you out of my mouth." I think the message is clear: The body of Christ needs to heat up.

I've discussed the benefits and costs of meanness at length. It is time to bring out the scales and weigh the decision to change or stay the same. On the benefits side of meanness, we have the emotional "feel good" or rush associated with being mean and the perception of earthly power. These outcomes benefit only the perpetrator. Costs are more far-reaching.

Costs to the perpetrator include distraction from caring and responding and, in the case of offensiveness or despicability, total derailment from the pursuit of Christ's likeness. Costs to the victim include embarrassment, hurt feelings, lower self-esteem, loneliness, and physical harm. I've also suggested that victims of meanness may become perpetrators, creating a harmful, perpetuating cycle. Finally, the faith—the cause of Christ—suffers when Christians are mean. The brand is tarnished, and the message appears inconsistent. The faith's appeal to others is lost. Meanness costs the faith potential followers and denies people the benefits of Christ in their lives.

When a pitcher is tiring, you'll often see play stop and a conference occur at the pitcher's mound. The catcher, several infielders, and the pitching coach will huddle around the pitcher. The discussion can go several directions. The pitcher might simply be encouraged to hang in there, to throw strikes or throw away from a particular hitter. More often, however, the meeting allows another pitcher, often the closer, to warm up in the bull-pen, leading to an eventual pitching change.

It's time for a change. Time for Christians to be all in—in baseball terms, to bring in the Closer. Our world is spiraling out of control. Hate, exclusion, and intolerance are rampant. It seems as if Christians are in the field making errors while meanness is scoring at will.

Let's commit to pursuing Christ's likeness genuinely. I honestly believe the "best stuff" of Christians—the result of lives changed cathartically by Jesus—is enough to end any meanness rally. What do you say?

Chapter 6

Contemplating Change

At a baseball game, there comes a time when fans take a break and players size up where they stand before the contest moves into its critical final phase. Baseball fans refer to this as the seventh-inning stretch. As far as this book goes, we're there. Part of the title is "Finding Our Way Back to Christ's Likeness." We're about to start down that path by speaking of change, but before we do, what are our takeaways up to this point?

Thus far, I've described individual and corporate Christianity as the pursuit of Christ's likeness, and I've provided six aspirational "Jesus" themes for living and one overarching reality that makes the Christian life possible—Jesus' authority. I've stated that the pursuit of a Christlike life should be both cathartic and uncomfortable, as it challenges us to live in ways counter to the values of this world.

I introduced Christian meanness as an old phenomenon that has recently gained strength, leading to divisiveness within the body of Christ and seriously damaging the work and appeal of the faith. I've explored causes and costs of mean Christianity in an effort to build a case for change.

So we are metaphorically huddled at the pitcher's mound, deciding what to do next. Too many of us aren't throwing our best stuff. As I suggested in Chapter 5, it's time for the Closer. The remainder of this book examines four critical concepts: change, forgiveness, grace, and mercy. Let's think of these as pitches we all need to master—to accept, understand, and use. The good news is that our Coach has ultimate authority. We're not in this game alone.

CHANGE AS THE GATEWAY
TO A CHRISTLIKE LIFE

Change—now that's an uncomfortable word. Let's just be honest: We don't like it. Change is usually suggested because we've failed or haven't been as successful as we or others would like. Seldom do we change for change's sake. I've suggested that when it comes to meanness, Christians must change, because the costs of not doing so are simply too high.

How does constructive change happen? I'm not sure there is a simple answer. Lots of things can lead to positive change. Real change in my life has typically started with an epiphany, moved to action, built strength with personal determination, coexisted with failure, and required lifelong commitment.

CHANGE MOTIVATED BY EPIPHANY

Most of us can identify a specific moment when we realized something about our life had to change. One of my more remarkable "change" epiphanies occurred around the time I took my first job. In Chapter 1, I shared that I accepted the position to be near a woman I was dating at the time and that shortly after starting the job, she ended the relationship. What I omitted was my initial reaction to the breakup. I was really down. For a period of time, I just mailed life in. After a week or two, I distinctly remember waking up one morning and saying, "Bill, you are being foolish." I'm convinced that anyone near me could have seen the light bulb over my head. My epiphany was that obvious—kind of like the moment in an action movie when the seemingly defeated star rises to respond. In this brief "ah-ha" moment, life changed for me. The day brightened and new opportunities seemed boundless.

I'm sure you have similar stories. Maybe it is about kicking a stubborn and unproductive habit, embracing or ending a relationship, or committing to a life dream. Why do productive epiphanies happen? Maybe we weigh the costs of continuing down destructive paths, and eventually the need to change becomes obvious. For those who embrace God's authority in their lives, I think there is more. I really believe that God wants good things for us. Jer 29:11 says, "'For I know the plans I have for you,' declares the Lord, 'plans to prosper you and not to harm you, plans to give you hope and a future.'" I believe in a heavenly Father who sees us off His path and is not averse to nudging us, sometimes gently and other times more forcefully, to change.

Have you been nudged in your life? Maybe it was a word from a friend, a Bible verse, or a sermon message that stirred your heart? Maybe simple quiet time with Him in His beautiful creation has moved you. I pray that this book can be a vehicle for God's nudging for Christians struggling with meanness. For me, God's nudges have been most effective when my heart was right, when I was doing my best to live like Jesus. I think a heartfelt and prayerful commitment to a Christlike life sets Christians up for wonderful life-changing epiphanies.

Of course, it doesn't have to be that subtle. Sometimes nudging can take a more obvious form. As I pondered how to pivot this book away from meanness and toward change, it dawned on me that the New Testament provides *the* prototypical example of meanness transformed. Remember Saul in the book of Acts? He was *the* champion persecutor of the Christian faith, *the* enabler as an angry mob killed Stephen, an early follower (Acts 7:54–60). As Saul set out on his personal crusade to end Christianity, Jesus nudged him, right? That's an understatement. For Saul, soon to become Paul, nudging took the form of a blinding personal encounter. Oh, but how that epiphany yielded change.

For the mean Christian, I guess God has more than one way to change a heart. Personally, I'd opt for openness tied to that personal commitment to live like Jesus. What do you think?

ACTION IN RESPONSE TO NUDGING

So, we get that nudge. What next? This one is simple—we either change or we ignore God's leading. I've ignored my share of nudges. Years ago, I remember feeling a very strong urge to speak with a mentor about faith. I was a student at the time, and this nudge seemed so out of left field that I suppressed it. After all, school and faith were in different compartments back then. I've regretted failing to respond ever since.

A more recent example of struggling with a nudge from God has been the writing of this book. I mentioned in Chapter 1 that the urge was strong this time—it kind of hit me like a brick. That said, I stalled a bit. I told my wife that I'd wait until I had more time to devote to the project. The longer I waited, the more He insisted. I got the message and got busy.

Let's take this back to meanness and assume that something you've read here or maybe heard elsewhere is nudging you toward a change epiphany. It is true that by ignoring this call and continuing your life unaffected you'll avoid the possible discomfort and transformation of change. Indeed, things will remain status quo, including those aspects of your life where meanness reigns. We've considered the costs of this path. Hopefully, you'll choose change.

As nudging leads to change, what will be your first action step? I'm fairly sure it is reconnection with your Maker—a little honest dialogue about where you are and where you want to be with His help. Maybe this could start with rededication within your prayer life and a call to an intentional walk daily. The chapters that follow discuss action steps more completely—specifically those that involve receiving and offering forgiveness, grace, and mercy.

The first step of action is often the most difficult. It's funny how the steps that follow usually occur with less caution. I remember watching my children take first steps. There was always that initial visible unsteadiness and those looks of apprehension. Once the first foot dropped, however, the steps that followed occurred in rapid succession. For many of us, it is time to let that first step of action drop—to begin in earnest a change journey from meanness to Christ's likeness.

CHANGE INFORMED BY STRENGTH AND PERSONAL DETERMINATION

When we're on a life-changing journey that truly mirrors Jesus, there will be challenges. If meanness has a significant foothold, Christians will need to confront and alter some firmly held assumptions. Most of us have constructed logical rationale to support our life decisions and actions. Our resulting belief systems may have even clouded our eyes to meanness. If we have been mean, we've likely not recognized it, or we've convinced ourselves that our actions are just, if not consistent with God's plan for our lives.

The epiphany of needed change and the initial action to live differently will certainly be followed by the realization that we must see the world differently—through Jesus' eyes. An earnest effort to seek God's heart in all matters will go a long way toward this end. We will, however, need to persevere, through personal strength and determination.

On August 18, 1967, Tony Conigliaro, an up-and-coming star for the Boston Red Sox, stood at the plate to face Jack Hamilton of the California Angels.[1] Tony was twenty-two years old and had already hit 102 homeruns in his young career with the Sox. In one brief second, a rogue fastball hit the left side of Tony's face, cracking his cheekbone, dislocating his jaw, and seriously damaging the retina of his left eye. Tony was out of baseball for the remainder of 1967 and all of the 1968 season. He returned in 1969, hitting fifty-six homeruns over the next two years. Tony Conigliaro's baseball life was cut short by his visual problems, but the strength and determination evident in his return to the game inspired many.

Tony Conigliaro could have left baseball for good after his horrific injury at the plate. Instead, he came back strong, determined to play again. My guess is that this resonates with readers of this book. Most of us have had times in our lives when we pushed through against the odds. As Christians move away from meanness in our lives, we'll have to be strong and determined. Old life patterns will surface. Rationales justifying meanness will return.

The good news is that our strength and determination have an authoritative source. The God who created this world, parted the seas, healed the sick, and raised the dead can certainly be your source of strength during a change journey. Amazingly, all we have to do is lean in a bit and submit to His authority. One of the earliest songs I learned on the guitar was "Learning to Lean" by John Stallings[2]. The chorus says it all.

> Learning to lean, I'm learning to lean,
> Learning to lean on Jesus,
> Finding more power than I've ever dreamed,
> I'm learning to lean on Jesus.

Lean in when you need the strength and determination to continue with change. Our Creator has strong shoulders.

CHANGE COEXISTING WITH FAILURE

When we set out to change, I can guarantee one thing: we'll take two steps forward and one step back. Failing along the way is a part of most change journeys.

1. Bruce Fitzpatrick, *The Tony Conigliaro Story* (United States: CreateSpace, 2011).
2. "Learning to Lean," Lyrics by John Stallings (1976), Imperial Records.

We've all experienced change efforts in which initial success is followed by setbacks. Maybe a diet runs into a dessert that can't be resisted; or an exercise program, once so consistent, is disrupted by an unexpected schedule change. On more than one occasion, I have committed to change in my spiritual life only to be discouraged with my inability to follow through. Periodic failures that keep us off the path of change can be disheartening. Too often, life's little failures keep us from even considering change. Our past struggles leave us sitting in life's dugout, out of the game and disappointed with ourselves. Instead of pushing for new possibilities, we surrender to the status quo.

Remember that one of the Jesus themes in Chapter 2 was "Jesus sets a high bar for living." I suggested that the life of Christ should be inspirational for Christians—we should push ourselves into areas where there may be little comfort and much sacrifice. Rather than wanting us in the dugout, Jesus wants us in the game. He knows that failures will come and that there will be lows as we strive to change. After all, Jesus lived this life in human form. I think He is more interested in the effort we offer than the setbacks we encounter. He wants our change journey to be continuous.

There are few things like succeeding in spite of failure—continuing to push through even when the victories seem few and far between. In relation to meanness, we can expect even our best God-informed efforts at change will sometimes fail. We will, on occasion, be selfish, petty, and possibly even harsh or despicable with others. The question is whether we will succeed after these failures. Will we strive to push forward and leave meanness behind?

I think of the ballplayer in the field who drops a fly ball in the most critical point of a game. Although his confidence may be shaken, the best players want another ball hit their way. They want a shot at redemption.

I promise you, there will be many opportunities to be mean as you pursue your change journey. When you fail and act in meanness, my advice is to pray for a shot at redemption. Ask God to give you the opportunity to make old failures right and the strength to "make the play" the next time around. I've said this before, but it's worth repeating: You are not in this alone. God is pretty good at the change game. Again, we just need to lean in and let Him lead.

CHANGE AND LIFELONG COMMITMENT

Changing forever—a laudable goal, but is it achievable? I think so. Before I go too far, let's clarify: Are we talking about instant change? You know, the kind that happened when Clark Kent entered the phone booth, only to return seconds later as Superman? While God is capable of changing us instantly and forever, for most of us, it's more like He's sitting on His porch whittling. The final product will be a masterful work created in His image. To get there, however, there will be some cuts and rough edges.

I guess I'm saying change is typically a process for Christians. Earlier in this book, I used Paul's words to describe the Christian life as a journey. Journeys have crooked and straight roads. Christians pursuing Christ's likeness travel them all. Two things will lead us home: His guidance and our commitment.

As I look back over this chapter, I notice a recurring theme. Change, the forever kind, requires His guidance. I've discussed being "in the zone" with God and how that readies us to care and respond. The bottom line is that being in that zone is central to every part of the Christian life, including change. How do we get there? How do we find ourselves so responsive to God that we operate in tandem with Him?

My dad used to describe riding a mule as a young boy in rural Mississippi. Dad said he got to know his mule so well that it not only responded to his verbal commands—"Gee!" and "Haw!"—but also to his movements. My father was so "in the zone" with his mule that he could simply lean one way or another and the animal would turn as directed. How did that happen? My guess is dad fed, cared for, and loved that mule. A relationship grew, and communication and guidance became second nature.

Can God guide you by simply leaning or with a subtle nudge? In Chapter 5, I described Christians as either all in, striving, compartmentalized, or claimers. The truth is, we move back and forth throughout these levels of "God-connectedness" during our lives. I honestly believe, however, that it is only when we are "all in" that we become an extension of God, fully responsive to His guidance.

I've been all in a few times in my life. While no specific formula may get you there, for me, "all in" times coincided with reflection on His word and prayer. Like my dad with his mule, when I was all in, God was feeding me, and I was communicating with Him. If you want lifelong change, let me suggest some time on your knees. His guidance will follow.

Something else that makes change a lifelong outcome is a personal commitment to a new life in Christ. We are committed to so many worthless things. Currently, I'm committed to learning how to play the guitar more formally (right now, I play by ear). I look forward to lessons with a classically trained guitarist, and I work hard to learn what he teaches me.

What are your commitments? Are you pursuing wealth, material things, new skills, another language? Where are you focusing your time? My guess is that we could all benefit from some reprioritization, especially as we strive to eliminate meanness from our lives.

I don't intend for this book to have altar-call overtones. I sat through many of those with fidgety feet and sweaty palms. That said, I can't overemphasize the importance of working to be all in with God. Committing to do so will be the best decision of your life.

As this chapter ends, I'm drawn again to the example of Paul (in Acts). It strikes me that Paul's life epitomizes change as I've described it here. His Damascus road experience provided the epiphany that started it all. After only three days, Paul moved straight to action and a life of incessantly preaching the gospel of Christ. To say his change was informed by strength and personal determination is an understatement. Paul became one of the most influential Christians in history, establishing churches throughout the known world and authoring many of the books of the New Testament. Although we don't read of many specific examples, I am certain that Paul experienced setbacks on his change journey—surely his meanness occasionally surfaced. We know, for example, that he was challenged within certain personal relationships (with Barnabas [Acts 15:36–41] and with Peter [Gal 2:6–10]). Paul was human like us, but all in as a Christian. His struggles paled in comparison to his successes.

Finally, Paul's change was lifelong. Until his death, he leaned in and followed Jesus, probably as much as anyone in recorded history.

What would have happened if Paul had continued his life as Saul? How severely would he have damaged the early church with his fervent pursuit of Christians? How many individuals would have never heard the gospel? Change is important—especially when it comes to meanness. In 2 Cor 5:17 we learn: "Therefore, if anyone is in Christ, he is a new creation. The old has passed away; behold, the new has come." Being Christlike requires change!

As I began this chapter, I had us huddled at the pitcher's mound. We were contemplating a change, thinking of bringing in the Closer. The chapters that follow share three core attributes of a changed Christian—forgiveness, grace, and mercy. I've said we can think of these as our "go-to" pitches. We need to explore these attributes as ones we both experience and offer to others—Christlike actions to fill the void of meanness in our lives.

The Coach just nodded to the bullpen, and now here comes the Closer. He has the "right stuff" and wants to be there beside you as this meanness rally ends. As He throws a few warm-up pitches, it's time for a decision. Are you "all in" this game or not? It's your call.

CHAPTER 7

Forgiveness

Re-dos, oh how I've wished for them. We've all had times when we've missed an opportunity or known we could have done better. For Christians trying to live like Jesus, failures come every day. Failing repeatedly wears you down. You begin to doubt. Discouragement sets in.

Long ago I accepted Jesus' authority in this world and in my life. Part of that authority is centered in His ultimate sacrifice for me on the cross and His victory over death. As a Christian, I know He did what He did so I could have re-dos in my life. His life, death, and resurrection allow me to live with failures, knowing He has the authority to forgive me. When I fail, all I have to do is ask for His forgiveness and receive His grace. You see, God's perfect fellowship is only available through forgiveness and grace. It may seem crazy, but this is all free for the asking.

This chapter and the next are about forgiveness and grace, cornerstones of the Christian faith. When embraced, these concepts are liberating catalysts for the Christian life journey. Forgiveness and grace are simple ideas, yet they challenge Christians to the core. Too many of us just don't feel worthy of the new life they provide.

This chapter addresses forgiveness. What is it, and why do we need it? Why do we find forgiveness so difficult to ask for and accept? How can it become easier? Can we take forgiveness too far? How should being forgiven change us? With these questions answered, we can examine the role forgiveness plays in changing the hearts and lives of mean Christians.

UNDERSTANDING FORGIVENESS

What Is Forgiveness?

Forgiveness is the process of forgiving and forgetting. Synonyms include *pardon* and *absolution*. It's a circular act. That is, we ask for forgiveness from those we offend and offer it to those who offend us. To be forgiven or to forgive epitomizes the notion of re-do. It creates a clean slate.

While we may be able to wrap our heads around the idea of forgiving, forgetting is more difficult. We hold on to memories of hurting others or being hurt. If we really want re-dos in life, however, we must forget both our forgiven transgressions and the transgressions perpetrated against us. Failing to do so leaves us open to revisiting and acting on the past. We'll explore forgetting more as we consider forgiveness in the Christian life.

Forgiveness, whether we are asking for it or receiving it, establishes "right" relationships with others—relationships unmarred by discord and characterized by mutual respect and cooperation. I think of the beauty of watching a team work together on the baseball diamond as they turn a double play. Televised games allow for slowed replay, showing the intricate and tandem movements of players as they adjust their positions on the field and execute their jobs to perfection. What replay doesn't show are the countless times players repeat these movements in practice. They have complete confidence that teammates will be at the right place at the right time. In fact, the ball is often thrown to a spot, assuming the player will arrive in time to make the play. The best teams illustrate right relationships in that they function together seamlessly. Forgiveness, in its purest form, allows for seamlessness in relationships—lives completely in sync with each other. One might question if this pure form of forgiveness is even possible.

Forgiving and forgetting is a tall order. I don't know how it can be accomplished without Christ. For me, positive and productive human relationships flourish when I am in a "right" relationship with my heavenly Father. Only when I have received forgiveness from Him can I ask for and receive it from others.

Forgiveness in the Christian Life

For Christians, everything starts with forgiveness. We realize that life is askew and that regardless of our best efforts, we are sinful. What is sin? To me, it's anything that keeps a person from an "all in" relationship with God. Sin varies for all of us. For some, it might be the headlong pursuit of wealth or power. For others, sin can relate to pride, envy, obsessions, behaviors, or even thoughts.

I believe that God nudges us to recognize sin in our lives. Unfortunately, we often become calloused if not overtly resistant to His leading. Truly trying to live like Christ is a great way to awaken to sinfulness. I know that times when I've been genuinely dedicated to His path, my sins have become most obvious to me.

You may be saying, "Bill, why bring up sin?" Christians will never be "all in" with persistent sin in their lives. Remember, God seeks a right and perfect relationship with us. He wants us to be so in tune that we (God and us) act in tandem, becoming His hands and feet in this world. Sin is *the* obstacle to this kind of relationship, and forgiveness is *the* solution.

For Christians, forgiveness begins as an act between us and God. In Chapter 2, I spoke of my belief in the triune nature of God—God the Father, God the Son (Jesus), and God the Holy Spirit. God the Father offers forgiveness to those who seek it because God the Son lived and died for each of us. God the Holy Spirit, among other things, keeps us constantly aware of our need for forgiveness with those nudges or reminders of sin in our lives.

The bottom line is that all Christians should find themselves in the ongoing process of rooting out sin through the vehicle of forgiveness. Forgiveness, as God designed it, is an elegant plan.

I also spoke of the need to forget. Forgetting includes moving beyond both what you have done to others and what others have done to you. For Christians, forgetting is possible (though admittedly challenging) because of God's example. Isa 3:25 says, "I, even I, am He who blots out your transgressions, for My own sake, and remembers your sins no more." With reference to Jesus' sacrifice for each of us, Heb 8:11 states, "Their sins and lawless acts I will remember no more." In sum, God has done it for us, and we must do it for others.

When a baseball player makes an egregious error during a game, his fellow players have to move on to the next play. Failing to do so will likely lead to more mistakes and ultimately the loss of the game. Teammates have to forget bad plays. The only way for us to forget our own transgressions and the offenses of others perpetrated against us is to focus on Christ and the forgiveness He constantly offers.

Finally, we must remember that forgiveness is no cavalier act. As a child I recited rote prayers asking for forgiveness. This was good practice in that it got me in the habit of praying, but I failed to understand the true nature of forgiveness. When Christians ask for God's forgiveness, He expects our best effort to turn from our old behaviors. More failures may follow, and forgiveness continues to be available, but we are obligated to do our part to change, to repent. We are to prove our repentance with our deeds (Acts 26:20).

So, we need forgiveness to be in right relationship with others. For Christians, this all starts with God. Right relationships allow us to be like Christ. We've now clearly shifted our focus to the second part of this book—finding our way back to Christ's likeness. In Chapter 6, I used the baseball analogy to suggest that we need to learn some basic pitches to live like Jesus. Once we decide to change our lives (pitch one), we must focus on forgiveness (pitch two).

Why Is Forgiveness So Difficult?

Forgiveness is hard. I think it runs counter to our nature as humans. We've arrived at this point as a species by taking care of "number one." In doing so, we've learned to be aggressive and protective when necessary. When someone strikes out at us, we strike back.

I can't help thinking of recent events in which a national leader, upon feeling offended, struck back with harsh comments about those who criticized him. Those in the leader's camp defended his actions: "When he is hit, he hits back ten times harder." Don't we all feel like this? When we are hit, don't we want to hit back? In this particular situation, I wonder what the national dialogue would have been if the leader had offered forgiveness rather than a vitriolic response. It is possible that one reason we don't forgive is that we're not really programmed to be forgiving. Are there other reasons?

For me, it is mostly about pride. I am prideful enough to think that I don't make many mistakes. You only need forgiveness when you mess up, right? I'm all good if my offenses are righteous. Pride takes us down a slippery path. In fact, it blinds us to our faults, to our need to be forgiven.

Being prideful can build a wall between you and your sin. Think about it: If you always see yourself as righteous, you never see yourself as out of step with God. I don't know about you, but I'm out of step much too often.

I have no reason to be prideful and every reason to be forgiven. I say this, yet pride challenges me daily.

Pride not only blinds us to the need for forgiveness, it keeps us from forgiving others. When we've been wronged, we can claim the moral high ground and say we will not forgive. Once again, our prideful position can keep us from accepting the forgiveness others offer. Frankly, it can make forgetting pretty difficult, too.

Independence can complicate forgiveness as well. In our culture, we value independence. Even as children, we want to "do it ourselves." But fierce independence leaves us on an island, solely responsible for the things we do wrong as well as what we do right. When on that island, it is pretty easy to rely stubbornly on ourselves after mistakes. At this point, independence breeds pride, and the probability of pursuing forgiveness becomes increasingly remote.

There is at least one more barrier to forgiveness. Too often we enjoy our position within damaged relationships, and some revel in their attempts to hurt others. They are quite satisfied with the pain they cause and actually find pleasure in their actions. What I'm describing comes from a different place than our aggressive, protective, or independent nature. It is not necessarily related to pride, either. It's simple meanness. When we are mean and enjoy it, we don't want to be forgiven, and we certainly don't want to change.

Enjoying one's position within a damaged relationship can hamper both sides of forgiveness. As described above, it can keep us from seeking forgiveness, but it also can prevent us from forgiving others. I've certainly wanted to wade a while in the pool of self-pity before even considering forgiving someone. I'm guessing you have as well.

Making Forgiveness Easier

For Christians, forgiveness comes more easily only as we make an intentional effort to draw closer to God. I've spoken of my personal actions in this regard—a dedicated prayer life and a conscious effort to be available on the life paths of others.

Without a doubt, my closest friend on this earth is my wife. Every day, we talk and laugh with each other, and I can honestly say our relationship is more devoted now than when we met thirty years ago. Why? We work on it. I don't mean we start our days strategizing about how we can love each other more. We simply talk and listen to each other. We care about each other's lives, both our ups and our downs.

What does making the effort to draw close to someone do for us? It creates a friend, a person you can go to without judgment. If, as Christians, we are in a close daily walk with our Maker, we're building a relationship that makes the subject of forgiveness easier to broach. Remember, He seeks a relationship with us. When describing God's desire for a loving relationship, 1 John 4:10 states that "In this is love, not that we loved God, but that He loved us. . ." *He loved us first*. Given His desire to know and love us, don't you think He stands constantly ready to offer forgiveness?

Central to drawing closer in a relationship is the concept of "working on it." Repetition is a key to acquiring a new skill. Baseball players throw warm-up pitches and take batting practice for a reason. They want the repetitions. They want to refine their play, and they know "practice makes perfect."

In an earlier section of this chapter, I noted that when we need to ask for forgiveness, we are often reluctant—our pride and independence get in the way. How can we move past this? What about a little practice? It can start in our prayer life. For quite a while I've used a prayer format that includes, among other things, a focus on confession and forgiveness. By talking to God about my need for forgiveness daily, I get in my practice. My guess is that most of us also have a few personal relationships in which practice could occur as well, where we know a request for forgiveness will be met with a loving response. Even though you might be on solid ground with your practice partner, the need for forgiveness is pretty ubiquitous. I've mentioned my wife and our relationship. Though we are close, I'd venture to say there is room for me to ask for her forgiveness daily.

There is one more thing that makes forgiveness easier: God's grace. Understanding the depth of His grace changes everything. We'll explore this more in Chapter 8.

CAN WE TAKE FORGIVENESS TOO FAR?

The simple answer is no. In Matt 18:21, Jesus notes that the accepted religious imperative to forgive one's brother seven times is insufficient: "I tell you, not seven times, but seventy times seven times." Do the math—that is 490 times! I think He was making a point, right? We are to forgive continuously, without limits.

There are, however, seldom simple answers for difficult questions. People often find themselves in harmful (even dangerous) relationships in which the continued offer to forgive perpetuates a cycle of abuse and/or violence. Remember that forgiveness, in its purest form, does not occur in isolation. It is offered under the assumption that the perpetrator will change. Earlier, I referred to this as repentance.

It is up to each of us to offer forgiveness both generously and with expectations. In doing so, there may be situations in which wrongdoers fail to alter their behaviors and, accordingly, relationship changes are necessary.

I've heard it said that we can only really change ourselves. In a relationship where forgiveness is offered and the offending party makes no effort to reform, the act of change falls to the person who was hurt. That is, it is up to the offended individual to change the nature of the relationship—by ending it or establishing new boundaries. This doesn't mean that forgiveness has not occurred. We can forgive others without enabling them to continue destructive life patterns.

Sometimes offenses are so senseless that forgiveness seems impossible. When there is no remorse or repentance in an unimaginably painful act, Christians have a unique opportunity. They can act in a manner inconsistent with this world, yet true to God's example of forgiveness and grace.

On June 17, 2015, a young gunman entered a church in Charleston, South Carolina, and took the lives of nine people participating in a prayer service. The shooter admitted to the killings and suggested he had acted to incite a race war. (He was Caucasian, and his victims were all African Americans.) At the shooter's court hearing, the victims' relatives had the opportunity to speak. One by one, each offered forgiveness. The watching world was stunned by this unexpected turn. These Christians, by all expected standards, could have responded in understandable rage, or even meanness, yet they opted to forgive. How could that happen? My guess is that these relatives had received God's pardon in their own lives. They knew the liberating nature of forgiveness.

HOW SHOULD FORGIVENESS CHANGE US?

Forgiveness provides a new start. In a baseball double header, the outcome of the first game has no bearing on the second. A team can lose by ten runs in game one, and the scoreboard—runs, errors, all of it—is wiped clean for game two. Teams get a fresh start—new opportunities in the field and at the plate.

This clean slate can be difficult to accept. You see, although I've suggested forgetting is a part of true forgiveness, we are human, and we hold on to pain, pain we have caused and pain we have endured. When we let transgressions go, though, new possibilities abound. For perpetrators, a clean slate means a chance to get things right—to live like Jesus. What joy this should evoke! I remember how Ebenezer Scrooge responded in Dickens' *A Christmas Carol* once he awoke from his dreams of Christmas past, present, and future.[1] Scrooge threw open his window and shouted Christmas greetings to all who passed. Shouldn't a forgiven Christian show similar joy?

How should the individual accepting the request for forgiveness respond? First, assuming the offer is heartfelt and accompanied by the honest intent to change, celebration should ensue. I may be overly optimistic, given the sensitive nature of many offenses, but at the least, there should be great relief—relief not only with the resolution of a wrongdoing but with the possibility of establishing that "right" relationship referred to earlier in this chapter. Second, I think those offended should feel appreciation. Asking for forgiveness is not easy. We all know this. Recognizing just how difficult asking for forgiveness is seems appropriate.

The beauty of forgiveness is it's always there for you. In fact, the constant availability of God's forgiveness seems to be an obstacle to some. They just can't understand a deal this good—there has to be a catch, right? There is no catch. God is this good.

Remember, however, forgiveness is not cheap. God is always willing to forgive, but He expects our best efforts to grow and change. As I've said before, life is a journey. There will be crooked and straight paths. Thank goodness we have God's forgiveness as our walking stick.

THE ROLE OF FORGIVENESS IN THE LIVES OF MEAN CHRISTIANS

We talked about forgiveness both in a more general sense and as it applies to Christians. Let's shift our thoughts to the role of forgiveness for the mean Christian. The first point is obvious: Meanness is sin.

---

1. Charles Dickens, *A Christmas Carol* (London: Chapman and Hall, 1843).

I've referred to sin as that which separates us from God. I've also suggested that sin may vary for each of us. That is, what is sinful or creates separation from God in my life may not in yours. Wealth is a good example. Wealth prevents some Christians from being "all in," while others may use their wealth as a tool for God's purposes. You'll remember very early in the book I stated that judgment is not my business, nor do I think it is the business of other Christians. I mention this because it is not my role to identify universal sins—doing so is judgment. This said, some sins are glaring, directly counter to the loving nature of God. Meanness is one of them.

In Chapter 3, I defined a mean Christian as someone who claims Christ yet at least some of the time treats others in petty, offensive, or despicable ways. I also noted that selfishness may motivate mean Christianity. I just don't see any way that petty, offensive, despicable, and selfish behaviors don't separate us both from God and others. Let's face it, being mean creates discord, and discord contributes to separation.

Some readers may continue to hang onto the idea that righteous indignation provides justification for meanness. Like the batter who strikes out repeatedly and blames it wrongly on the afternoon sun, indignation provides no excuse for being mean. Meanness is on us. Not only is it on us, but it's up to us to make things right.

I used Chapter 6 to reflect on change. I suggested that God the Spirit nudges us to show when change is needed. I also identified our commitment to a new life in Christ as central to readiness to change. For mean Christians, seeing meanness as sin likely will require something else: humility.

To be humble is to hold a lowly view of one's importance. Oh my, how I struggle with humility. Recently, my sweet and funny daughter used her *Star Wars* Yoda voice while pointing to me and said, "The vanity is strong in this one." I got a good laugh, but it is so true. I'm seldom humble. Why is this a problem?

Being humble puts us in a position in which we see the world as it really is—bigger and more important than we are. When we are prideful or vain, we have a hard time acknowledging any wrongdoing in our lives. Eph 4:2 says, "Be completely humble and gentle; be patient, bearing with one another in love." If we are completely humble, we are at the bottom of the totem pole of importance, always looking up. From that vantage point, it is much easier to see God's hand in the outcomes of our lives rather than our own.

What does humility have to do with forgiveness and meanness? As we seek humility, we lose our focus on self. This allows us to see ourselves as we are. If we take a humble attitude into an honest effort to live like Jesus, we'll be open to God's nudging on meanness and a host of other things in our lives.

So we see meanness as sin, what's next? The simple answer is to ask for forgiveness—first from God and then from those we've offended. Humility helps here. Without it, I'm not sure we could take this initial step toward forgiveness.

The "God part" of forgiveness is easiest for me. I guess that comes from seeing God as a loving Being, who seeks my fellowship and wants a "right" relationship. I'm not saying I'm good at asking for God's forgiveness or that my pride never gets in my way. I'm just saying that asking for His forgiveness is easier than asking others to forgive me.

I know this isn't true for everyone. I have a new friend who fought in Afghanistan. He has shared that he can't understand how God could forgive the things he did—things he was ordered to do as a soldier but seemed so unforgiveable. My friend feels unworthy of forgiveness. Although I can't begin to understand his pain and memories, I know God can forgive him. In 1 John 1:9 we learn that "If we confess our sins, He is faithful and just, and will forgive us our sins and purify us from all unrighteousness." Note the verse says *all* unrighteousness. Nothing is off the table here.

In sum, regardless of what you have done in the meanness arena, forgiveness from God is available for the asking. What about asking others to forgive you? In Eph 4:31–32, Paul encourages those who have been mean to get on with asking for forgiveness: "Get rid of all bitterness, rage and anger, brawling and slander, along with every form of malice. Be kind and compassionate to each other, just as Christ forgave you."

How do we ask others to forgive us? Again, humility helps. Approaching someone you have offended from a position of humility makes your request for forgiveness easier for them to accept. It gives you credibility and reflects a genuineness that opens the door to reconciliation. We all know this is not easy.

I have a hard time asking forgiveness for the little things—my anger over vegetable peelings in the sink, for example. The big things often seem unapproachable. My advice is prayer and practice. Goodness knows, we all have room for prayer and practice.

Thus far, I have primarily spoken of the more difficult side of forgiveness. But there is an upside as well. Remember I mentioned that I've longed for re-dos in my life. Re-dos are the upside to forgiveness. Really, it's more than just a re-do; it's that completely clean slate I mentioned earlier. Heb 8:12 says, "I will forgive their wickedness and remember their sins no more." God has forgiveness down pat—He forgives and forgets, and we get to start over.

While it is crystal clear that God provides a clean slate, others may struggle to forgive us as completely. When they do, however, their forgiveness gets us back on track to healthier relationships, relationships that eventually become as He intended, unmarred by discord and characterized by mutual respect and cooperation.

WHAT IF?

Several times throughout this book I've asked the question, "What if?" In doing so, I've tried to create scenarios for reflection. I think a few more are in order. Specifically, I'd like to return to a few of the examples of mean Christianity provided in Chapter 3 and ask, "What if?"

Let's begin with the example of Westboro Baptist Church (WBC). Remember, to express their belief that homosexuals are an "abomination" and the root of God's anger against America, members of this church have picketed at high-profile events, including funerals of soldiers and those killed by gun violence. The organization also maintains a website with hate-filled church positions and links to videos that disparage those who don't hold their views.

What if the leadership and members of WBC asked God for forgiveness for the hatred they have offered? What if the church re-worked their website to offer a sincere apology to the gay and lesbian community? What if WBC's leadership and members asked forgiveness from family members of dead service men and women and others they have offended? Could wounds begin to heal? Would the brand of Christianity benefit?

Let's take another example of very visible Christian meanness from Chapter 2—the Facebook page "Christians Against Illegal Immigration." This site disparages immigrants as "thieves" and "robbers" while warning of a diminishing "white" influence. It also speaks out against others who do not share views promoted by the site.

What if the authors of this site felt the nudging of the Holy Spirit regarding their meanness and asked God for forgiveness? What if they replaced their hate-filled page with a new site asking for forgiveness from those they had offended and speaking to the many positive contributions made by immigrants each day? What if their new site assisted visitors with obtaining citizenship? What would be the impact on site visitors? Would they see Jesus in the humility of those asking for forgiveness? Would they see Him in the helping hand extended to those in need?

"What ifs" can extend to the corporate Christian church as well. What if churches asked God to forgive them for the envy they show toward other growing and vibrant bodies of Christ? What if they asked forgiveness from those groups? What if the Christian church asked to be forgiven for exclusionary attitudes that shut people out from worship—individuals in poverty or those who represent different races, nationalities, cultural backgrounds, religious traditions or sexual orientations? What if these requests for forgiveness were offered publicly?

These acts of forgiveness would not only mirror the life of Jesus, they would be Christian brand-changers. The world would see a church that resembles the Deity it follows.

If we move our "what if" question to the world of individual mean Christians, what could happen? For example, what if each of us who gossips asked for God's forgiveness and sought the forgiveness of those we offended? What if, after offering harsh or mean language in person or through social media, we asked for God's forgiveness and requested forgiveness from those who may have heard or read our comments? What if those who have been so selfish with their pursuit of resources asked God for forgiveness and used their time and material wealth for His kingdom?

I think the outcomes of these individual acts of forgiveness may have as big an impact as the larger ones mentioned earlier. Person by person, the world would change, and we would all move a little closer to a Christlike life.

Shouldn't that be what it's all about anyway? Shouldn't we do everything in our power to live like Jesus? Remember, I described Christianity in corporate and individual terms as the emulation of Christ. We'll never get there with sin in our lives. We'll never reflect His love, compassion, humility, and inclusive nature as long as meanness persists.

I know some of you are saying that this kind of change can never happen, or that we are incapable of radical transformation. You're right, *we* alone are incapable. If left to our own devices, *we* will pursue the course of meanness; *we* will fail to offer forgiveness when offended. But there is another way: God's elegant plan of forgiveness.

In 1993, Mary Johnson lost her son to a senseless act of gun violence. The shooter, Oshea Israel, was convicted of the crime and sentenced to twenty-five years in prison. Initially, Mary was among the loudest voices calling for Oshea's imprisonment. She wanted justice. Over time, Mary's position changed. She felt God's overwhelming nudge to forgive Oshea and eventually worked for his release. Mary and Oshea now live in the same neighborhood and have established a loving friendship. Mary gives God the glory for her change of heart. Christ's example of forgiveness allowed her to forgive.

You are absolutely right when you say we can't forgive and be forgiven in a way that will change this world. I will not argue that point. The good news is that God can. He forgives and allows us to accept requests for forgiveness from others. God was there for Mary Johnson and is there for you—now and forever. Why shouldn't you be the one to get the ball rolling? You have His ear.

CHAPTER 8

Grace

It was Christmas morning 1978. I was a very tired twenty-one-year-old who had lost my childhood Christmas enthusiasm. All I really wanted to do was sleep. My family had a different plan. I remember my grandmother coming to my room repeatedly, telling me it was time to open presents. Eventually, I acquiesced. Crawling out of bed and stumbling down the stairs, I saw my parents, my sister and brother, and my grandmother assembled in our living room waiting for me. Everyone was smiling oddly.

Plopping down on the couch by my stocking, I began to slowly unpack its surprises. To my astonishment, my grandmother abruptly took the stocking from me and turned it upside down. The last thing that fell to the floor was the key to a new car. I was shocked. My parents were middle-class yet had always provided for me and my siblings generously. This, however, was beyond my expectations.

I did nothing to deserve that car. Nothing. It was an unmerited gift from my parents, a gift they offered at some sacrifice simply because they loved me. This is grace—undeserved favor. As I mentioned in Chapter 7, grace is a cornerstone of the Christian faith. Both mysterious and wonderful, grace provides a unique glimpse into God's true nature. You see, the source of God's grace is love—love that runs so deep it is offered freely and lacks conditions. In 1 John 4:8 we read, "Whoever does not love does not know God, because God is love."

When this book began to take shape, I saw the need for a chapter on grace. Christians, especially those struggling with meanness, desperately need clarity on grace. Consistent with the baseball examples throughout this book, the previous two chapters focused on "pitches" we must develop if we are to emulate Jesus. Grace is our third pitch. The very best pitchers typically have one defining throw. Grace is *it* for Christians. Not because it's easy, but because it is consistent with God's character—it's God's best stuff. Understanding, receiving, and applying God's grace are the keys to finding our way back to Christ's likeness.

What is God's grace, and why is it central to the Christian life? Is grace part of the natural human condition? Does it differ from forgiveness? How does the life of Jesus reflect grace as a model for us? Does its free nature cheapen grace as a gift? These are all questions worthy of exploration for Christians. Of course, for the purposes of this book, we are also interested in how grace can alter the lives of mean Christians.

UNDERSTANDING GRACE

God's Grace

I've heard sermons and hymns about God's grace my entire life. That said, I'm not sure I've ever tried to distill this concept to its core. Pondering God's grace is time well spent for any of us. It's really more than that—it's a necessity if we want to appreciate and reflect the essence of our Maker.

God's grace—His unmerited favor for us—when did all this start? I think grace was present in the creation event. I've always believed in an ever-present God, one who pre-dates time. Assuming this is the case, God's creation of this world and everything beyond it occurred as an act of un-merited favor for us, its inhabitants. Some have referred to this as "common grace"—grace available for humankind, simply seen and experienced by all throughout the lives we lead. Common grace is apparent to onlookers in the beauty of a sunset or in the face of a newborn child.

Creation is a wonderful illustration of God's grace, but no example is better than the gift of His Son. John 3:16 says, "For God so loved the world that he gave His one and only Son, that whoever believes in Him shall not perish but have eternal life." This is "saving grace." Grace available to all through its acceptance as a free gift.

Would you offer saving grace? I have a wonderful son. We don't always see eye to eye, but I love him deeply. I would not give him up willingly for anything. God's offer of His Son for you and me was the quintessential act of His grace. We did nothing—nothing—to deserve that.

Where does God's grace originate? I believe it is an extension of His love. He loves us so much that He offers continuous unmerited favor. As we deconstruct God's grace, then, we find the triune God, His love for us, and the grace He offers because of that love. God's love and its resulting grace are at ground zero for Christians.

God's grace is central to the Christian life because it makes everything else possible. Our existence as Christians is built upon God's love and grace.

Grace and the Human Condition

Let's imagine life characterized by unmerited favor—a grace-filled life. Do we see this in humanity? The simple answer is no. Our world's headlines of war, hatred, and separation suggest grace is inconsistent with the human experience. It is not that simple, though. I've seen examples of grace in humankind. Many involved non-Christians—individuals of other faiths or no faith at all who willingly offered grace to others. Is there something that makes grace possible regardless of faith? The answer is evident in the source of God's grace: His love. Loving individuals, regardless of their faith status, can and do offer grace to others.

Grace within human relationships is a byproduct of a deep and abiding love. Think of the parent who sacrificially gives for her child, the spouse or friend who forgoes his interests to promote those of another, or the soldier who loses her life so others can live. Without faith these things happen, but the truth is they occur much too infrequently.

In baseball and other sports, there are always glimpses of greatness—a towering home run or a diving catch in the field, brief windows revealing the very best a player can perform. For most of the game, we don't see this level of play. At best, greatness on the field comes only now and again.

The same can be said of human love and the grace it generates. We see it, but just not enough. If deep and abiding love leads to grace, increasing grace seems simple. More love should yield more grace. But here is the rub: Humans struggle to love one another. Sure, we offer love to those closest to us, but not to everyone. In fact, we often fail even to extend grace-generating love to those we care about the most.

For Christians, accepting and emulating Christ is the answer. As we lose ourselves in the pursuit of His likeness, love becomes our watchword. As He did, we live to love others—to care and respond. The more we love, the more we offer grace. The more we offer grace, the more we look like Him.

The "all in" Christian eventually finds himself or herself living a grace-filled life, providing unmerited favor at every turn. Although the potential for grace lies in all of us, the catharsis it ignites awaits our action. For the Christian, this is a commitment to follow Jesus.

If grace characterized every Christian, what a team we would field! Life would be one all-star, grace-filled play after another—unmerited favor in all of our relationships. Sounds ideal, doesn't it? It's possible, but it's not easy.

Grace and Forgiveness

These terms are often used synonymously. Are they different? I think so. Grace is a proactive act. God's grace existed before us and will continue well after we are gone. It is a constant truth of God that awaits our discovery and acceptance. Simply put, God has always offered His grace. I believe that once developed, grace can have something near that constant property for us as humans. That is, we can become people proactively characterized by grace. We will slip up but generally reflect His grace.

In comparison, forgiveness is reactive. God's elegant plan of forgiveness came after the onset of sin. He offered forgiveness in response to sin—forgiveness, though now a constant, wasn't always on the table. You know how forgiveness works. We do something that separates us from God and react by asking for forgiveness. Or, someone perpetrates an offense against us, and we react by forgiving.

In Chapter 7, I suggested that grace makes forgiveness easier. If we are already living a grace-filled life, a life of unmerited favor toward others, doesn't it make sense that forgiveness would be easier? However, the truth is that, as I have written many times, life is a journey. We aren't always grace-filled, and, accordingly, we perpetrate offenses against others and struggle with asking for and accepting forgiveness. The grace-filled life that makes forgiveness easier is aspirational, yet so worthy of pursuit.

I have one final comment about grace and forgiveness. There are times when forgiveness is offered after unimaginable moments of violence or abuse, when perpetrators have no remorse and don't ask for forgiveness. In Chapter 7, I shared the example of victims' families after the Charleston church shootings of 2015. Another comes from the popular book *The Shack*, in which a father eventually forgives his daughter's killer.[1] I suggested that this kind of forgiveness is rooted in the forgiveness experience; that is, those who forgive do so because they have experienced God's forgiveness. It likely goes a little deeper. This kind of forgiveness has to be informed by love and grace.

Aside from horrific events in which grace makes forgiveness more likely, there are the little struggles—things that divide families and can persist for years. Personal relationships often result in troubles in which one party is immovable in his or her position. I think grace can lead to forgiveness here as well. Remember, we only control change for ourselves. There will be instances when we have to offer forgiveness and move on with some things unresolved. A grace-filled life makes these times less painful.

Jesus and Grace

A study of the New Testament reveals that Jesus didn't use the word *grace*. In fact, in the canonical gospels the word *grace* appears only twice. Luke shares that the "grace of God" was on Jesus as a child (Luke 2:40), while John states, "For the law was given through Moses; grace and truth came through Jesus Christ" (John 1:17). Assuming Jesus is a part of the triune God and that God's love and grace are central to His nature, grace should be evident in all aspects of Christ. If He didn't use the word, what does the life of Jesus tell us about grace? We find the answer in His day-to-day existence—the stories He shared and how He lived each moment.

Jesus loved to speak through parables. In fact, forty-six recorded parables of Christ provide the structure by which He delivered much of His teaching. While Jesus frequently used a direct instructional method to share interpretation of the law with religious leaders (e.g., Matt 23:2–7), everyday followers heard parables. Many were filled with examples of unmerited favor. For example, in parables of the lost sheep and coin (Luke 15:1–10), unmerited favor is obvious—the coin and sheep represent those out of step with God who, through no actions of their own, are found. The parable of the Good Samaritan (Luke 10:29–36) is about the misfortune of a traveler who was robbed, beaten, and left for dead. While many people

1. William P. Young, *The Shack* (Nashville, TN: Faithwords Publishing, 2007).

passed by the injured traveler, a despised Samaritan stopped and tended to the man's welfare. The traveler, though a victim of undeserved actions himself, did nothing to warrant the Samaritan's favor. Finally, Jesus' parable of the prodigal son brings home a strong message of grace (Luke 15:17–24). A young man who had insisted upon, received, and squandered his portion of his father's wealth was welcomed home by his father with open arms and celebration. The son was undeserving of favor yet received it bountifully. Clearly, Jesus' teachings were grace-filled.

What About His Life?

His healings and other miracles come to mind. Did the woman who touched Jesus' garment do anything to deserve her healing (Luke 8:43–44)? How about those who were deformed, lame, deaf or dumb, blind, or had leprosy (Mark 3:3–5; Mark 2:11–12; Mark 7:32–35; John 9:1–12; Matt 8:3)? Did these individuals deserve His favor? What about the resurrections of the widow's son and Lazarus (Luke 7:11–17; John 11:38–44)? Did anyone involved in these events deserve Jesus' favor? Finally, did the wedding participants at Cana or the thousands who sought His teaching deserve to drink or to be fed (John 2:7–10; Matt 14:1621)?

All of the examples above and many others available in the gospels illustrate a grace-filled life in Jesus—a life of unmerited favor. Of course, it didn't end there. Jesus willingly accepted His cup of sacrifice, making the clearest statement of grace ever. He died for you and me. His ultimate action of grace was, is, and forever will be favor that we do not deserve.

Jesus was grace-filled, and if we live to emulate Him, we must be as well.

Is God's Grace Cheapened Because It Is Free?

All my life, I've heard giving things away cheapens them. This idea is certainly prevalent in the realm of business. A product with a low price is often assumed to be of lesser quality. Likewise, in my world of clinical services, free therapies or treatments are questioned as to their value.

I've suggested that the core essence of God is love and grace. I've also supported the idea that these attributes are constants. That is, there are no conditions for their availability to Christians and others. Finally, I've proposed that God's forgiveness is a byproduct of His love and grace, and that it, too, is freely available. I've offered my thought that forgiveness comes with no conditions, but that, once forgiven, we as Christians have a responsibility to press forward with a renewed resolve to live like Jesus—to repent and leave transgressions behind.

Does the free nature of God's grace, and for that matter His love and forgiveness, sound cheap to you? For a moment, think back to my discussion of Christian commitment—my use of the terms "claimers," "compartmentalized," "strivers," or "all in" to describe levels of investment when pursuing Christ's likeness. Remember I said that in reality, we likely drift in and out of these categories along our Christian journey. My guess is that claimers (those who claim Christ yet do not emulate Him) and compartmentalized Christians (those who pursue Christ only in isolated aspects of their lives) embrace cheap grace.

German theologian Dietrich Bonhoeffer offers a stinging description of cheap grace in his classic book *The Cost of Discipleship*.[2] Interestingly, he closely ties the concept of grace to forgiveness. Bonhoeffer suggests that those embracing cheap grace hear the gospel this way: "Of course you have sinned, but now everything is forgiven, so you can stay as you are and enjoy the consolations of forgiveness."[3] Bonhoeffer criticizes cheap grace because it does not demand discipleship.

Discipleship is critical. Disciples fervently follow those they revere. Remember theme seven from Chapter 2? Jesus says "Follow me." That doesn't mean to walk behind Christ, admiring His life from afar but not adopting it. To the contrary, it calls us to walk with Him—to live as He lived. When we as Christians busy ourselves with following Jesus, we come to understand costly grace. Bonhoeffer suggests, "Costly grace confronts us as a gracious call to follow Jesus, it comes as a word of forgiveness to the broken spirit and the contrite heart. It is costly because it compels a man to submit to the yoke of Christ and follow him; it is grace because Jesus says: 'My yoke is easy and my burden is light.'"[4]

God's unmerited favor is there for all of us. "All in" Christians don't do what they do to earn grace or due to a sense of indebtedness because God is gracious. They do what they do because they are following Him in pursuit of His likeness. God embodies love, grace, and forgiveness. So must we.

2. Dietrich Bonhoeffer, *The Cost of Discipleship* (New York: Macmillan, 1979).

3. Ibid., 48.

4. Ibid., 45.

The entire package of love, grace, and forgiveness does seem cheap without discipleship. You might have guessed that Bonhoeffer has been considered radical by many. Christianity *should* be radical. Several times in this book I've referred to the Christian life as both a cathartic and uncomfortable journey. It's not easy, but it is rewarding.

The Christian life is not lived from the sidelines. Could a baseball game occur if all the players stood in the dugouts or along the baselines? No. They have to be in the field. We have to be engaged with God in a lifelong journey that occurs moment to moment, day to day. This is a demanding path that calls us to live within a new paradigm—one inconsistent with this world and characterized by God's love, grace, and forgiveness.

There is a choice here. Christians can embrace cheap grace and never know the fullness of life possible in Christ, or we can take up our crosses and follow Him.

POTENTIAL IMPACT OF GRACE ON MEAN CHRISTIANITY

Costly grace is transformative. It calls us to a challenging level of discipleship. How might the body of Christ look if all Christians embraced costly grace? The themes of Christ generated in Chapter 2 provide a glimpse. We would all submit completely to His authority; care and respond with authenticity; live out values of selflessness, humility, love, compassion, kindness, and faith; hold a high bar for living that encourages our best. In sum, we would all be following Jesus. Not from afar but side by side.

Assuming all Christians pursued this path, what would happen to meanness? It would not exist. Our plates would be too full. The ultimate impact of God's grace on Christian meanness could be its eradication.

Again, I see you shaking your head and saying, "But we're human, and there is going to be meanness." Ok, let's say that, even if we're "all in," we fail some. Let's also recognize that we have God's elegant plan of forgiveness to get us back on track when we do. Can you envision a world full of Christians on a consistent path to live like Christ, who, though imperfect, keep striving and progressing? If so, what would be the impact on Christian meanness? Could we reduce it by five percent, by half, or by seventy-five percent?

My point? We can do much better. If as Christians we could simply grasp the completeness of God's love and grace, we would do so much better. How do we, then, as a body of Christ that includes mean Christians, begin to live in a way that reflects costly grace?

It all begins with pitch one—change. We have to recognize the need to alter our paths. I've suggested that recognizing the need for change is more likely if we are intentionally seeking a close fellowship with God. Define this as you like, but for most it means time and effort. Time to communicate with Him and effort to live like Jesus. That second part—living like Jesus—might well require some study. I'm pretty sure that many of us need to unlearn some things we've been told about Christ and, more specifically, Christianity. As I suggested in Chapter 3, the Christian Church has too often gotten off message by encouraging much of the meanness we see today. Let me recommend that you go back to the source—the canonical gospels—to learn about Jesus. I did this for you in Chapter 2, but I believe some personal study is worth your time. Truly knowing whom you follow can fuel your journey.

Step two of moving toward a grace-filled life is pitch two—forgiveness. Root out the meanness or other things that separate you from God. Make the commitment to live differently and, when you fail, do it all again. God can change you in an instant, or He can change you bit by bit. The ultimate outcome of either process is the likeness of Christ. We just have to keep moving forward.

This brings us to the problem of actually increasing grace in our lives—pitch three. I've suggested that more love equals more grace and that more grace equals less meanness. Sounds like God's love is the key. If we loved like God loves, we'd offer grace as He does as well, and meanness would be off the table. This seems like a tall order that necessitates achieving the unexpected.

In 1960, no one expected the Pittsburgh Pirates to beat the New York Yankees in the World Series. Throughout the seven-game series, the Yankees outscored the Pirates 55–27. Most observers saw the Yankees as the stronger team, yet the Pirates eked out four wins by a total of seven runs. The Pirates became the champs in what is widely considered to be one of the biggest upsets in World Series history.

The unexpected can happen. People can become more loving. Is there a critical point from which love can start? Recently, my wife attended a festival where people of many backgrounds and faiths grew close together. As a volunteer at the event, she drove speakers to and from local airports. On one occasion, she found herself in the car for a lengthy period with an individual of no faith, but their conversations just flowed. They found common ground in talking about personal interests and family.

Is it possible that common ground exists between mean Christians and those they victimize? Let's start at the very core of the human experience. The psalmist says, "I praise you because I am fearfully and wonderfully made; your works are wonderful . . ." (Ps 139:14). This verse suggests that each one of us as God's creation is fearfully and wonderfully made—that His work in creating mankind is wonderful. So where is our common ground? Could it be a realization that God doesn't make mistakes? That there are no rejects? That God made and loves each of us as we are?

I think our common existence as God's creations can be a starting point for care and respect when so much else about us differs. Recently, our polarized political spectrum came together when a congressman was shot during a benefit baseball practice. A few short weeks later the political divide briefly subsided when a senator was diagnosed with a life-threatening disease. In these cases, people who shared little within the sphere of politics recognized their common humanity and offered prayers and good wishes to colleagues in difficult circumstances.

What if those of us with an inclination to meanness saw our potential victims as God's creation, beautifully and wonderfully made? Let's put some faces to this question. Think of a first encounter with someone who is transgender, or gay or lesbian, or attired in clothing associated with the Muslim faith, or of a different race, or disabled, or disadvantaged, or on the other side of the political aisle? Where does your mind go? For many, fear takes over—fear of difference. Unfortunately, fear leads to avoidance at best and meanness at worst. What if, as an alternative, our first thought was, "The person standing in front of me is, like me, a part of God's creation, fearfully and wonderfully made"? Would this realization of our common ground open the door to a different reaction?

Maybe a "common-ground" epiphany is a place to start. I'm not saying it will always lead us to more love and grace, but I think it can. My recent experience with a group of friends of different religious backgrounds, nationalities, and cultures has been delightful. Our common human experience is leading us to a deepening sense of personal appreciation and affection.

I think of the beloved hymn by Herbert Woolston, "Jesus Loves the Little Children." The first verse says,

Jesus loves the little children,
All the children of the world,
Red and yellow,
Black and white,
They are precious in His sight,
Jesus loves the little children of the world.

These lyrics ring true and could be amended to include all forms of diversity. Have you watched children react to difference? They typically don't. Our reaction of fear is learned and can be unlearned with a little effort.

Common ground can go a long way to finding and spreading God's love and grace. Remember the parable about yeast and dough? In Matt 13:33 we learn, "The kingdom of heaven is like yeast that a woman took and mixed into about sixty pounds of flour until it worked all through the dough." The recognition of something common and good in another person can be a bridge to love and grace, something that starts in individual relationships and works its way through the fabric of our society.

Is there something else many of us have in common? Those who are Christians share Christ. No matter how deep the divisions are between you and others in Christ, Christians have Jesus in common. We may not see His gospel in exactly the same way, but we are saved by the same grace and called into the service of the same Master. We are joint heirs with Him (Rom 8:17), brothers and sisters in Christ. That should be *the* ideal starting point from which His love and grace can grow.

The next time you find yourself drifting toward meanness, remember the common ground we share with those different from us. Common ground is as central as our humanity or, in many cases, as important as our Lord. Common ground can be the nexus leading to His love, more grace, and an easier and more complete path to forgiveness.

I'm sure many of you have sung John Newton's "Amazing Grace" more than once. When we sing or say something repeatedly, it can become mundane. Take a moment to consider the lyrics carefully:

Amazing grace
How sweet the sound
That saved a wretch like me,
I once was lost, but now I'm found
Was blind, but now I see,
'Twas grace that taught my heart to fear

And grace my fears relieved,
How precious did that grace appear
The hour I first believed.

It's time for the Christian community to embrace God's unmerited favor, to remember how His grace appeared when we first believed, and to join together to live out costly grace as we follow Jesus. As challenging as this may seem, it really boils down to pursuing His likeness each day. In baseball terms, we just have to keep our eyes on the ball—or, in this case, on Him.

CHAPTER 9

Mercy

Have you ever heard of the mercy rule? In baseball, it's applied when one team builds an insurmountable lead late in a game. The rule frequently comes up in youth league play but is also used in college baseball if one team holds a ten-run advantage after seven innings, especially if the teams are playing the first game of a doubleheader. The mercy rule forces the team with the upper hand to end the contest. It offers mercy to the team that is behind.

Mercy is a nebulous term, often used synonymously with forgiveness and grace. To me, mercy shares qualities with these concepts but is unique. Like forgiveness and grace, it is something we receive and offer. But unlike those terms, mercy, especially our choice to extend it to others, most often occurs as an act with a definable moment. While forgiveness comes after contemplation, and grace should be more of an underlying constant construct in our lives, mercy typically requires an "in-the-moment" decision. For this chapter, we'll mostly consider the act of being merciful toward others.

Let's use a real-world characterization of mercy. My pastor recently defined it as what we do when we have the power to choose our actions. Think of it this way. It's how we respond when we have our proverbial foot on the neck of someone else.

Mercy is the final pitch we'll learn. It is critical because our opportunities to be merciful often occur without notice. Although there are times when offering mercy occurs after forethought (we'll later refer to this as preemptive mercy), chances to be merciful can also arrive with little warning, in the heat of a moment (referred to later as flashpoint mercy).

There comes a time when a baseball pitcher begins to lose his stuff, when a ninety-mile-per-hour fastball is beyond his physical capacity. Savvy pitchers don't quit the game. To the contrary, they develop a new pitch, something they can throw in place of the fastball of their youth.

Early in this book I took judgment—a go-to pitch for mean Christians—off the table. It's time to replace it. Our replacement pitch, the one that will carry us further on our journey to be like Christ, is mercy.

As with the pitches introduced in the last three chapters, reflecting on mercy raises questions worth considering. For example, what are the origins of God's mercy? Is being merciful a human or divine quality? If not innately human, how do we learn to be merciful? What does Jesus offer to assist us in our efforts to learn mercy? How does mercy fit into the love, forgiveness, and grace formula that informs the walk of "all in" Christians? Of course, we're left with the task of exploring the potential role of mercy (pitch four) in the lives of mean Christians.

UNDERSTANDING MERCY

Origins of God's Mercy

If grace is undeserved favor, mercy is an act of grace offered at a specific time when other alternatives are possible and may seem more appealing. Mercy, then, is a deliberate grace-filled act that flows counter to reason and expectation.

In God's grace, we receive something we don't deserve. With His mercy, we avoid what is deserved. To illustrate, I enjoy God's common grace when I sit on a nearby mountain and appreciate His handiwork. In contrast, I receive His mercy when I freely accept His salvation through Christ in spite of my sinful state. Simply put, I deserve a different outcome. Frankly, you do as well.

What is the source of God's mercy? It's His love and desire to be in right relationship with us. "Calling off the dogs"—literally altering the course of what is deserved—can only come from love. The depth of God's love is hard to grasp. Sure, we love, but our love is often tempered by what we perceive as right or just. Through human eyes, offenders deserve what they get. We embrace the old adage, "If you do the crime, you do the time."

Being merciful is a tall order, one that can only be followed as we delve deeper into a relationship with God that transforms us into His likeness.

Is Mercy a Divine or Human Quality?

This answer seems straightforward, especially after acknowledging that humans struggle with mercy. The truth, however, is a little murky. Similar to my comments about grace in Chapter 8, I know we have the capacity for mercy. That is, in fleeting and infrequent moments we all can offer an undeserving alternative to a deserved fate.

I was a pretty good kid, but I got in my share of trouble, mostly little things. When I was about nine or ten, I frequently rode my bicycle to a local pharmacy to look at comic books and toys. On one occasion, I discovered a water rocket for just a few dollars. For days, I dreamed of filling that rocket, pumping it up, and letting it fly. It became an obsession. I needed that rocket in the worst way, but I had one problem—I didn't have the money.

I knew of one place where money was there for the taking, a place where a few dollars might not be missed—my brother's coin collection. My brother kept books of old coins and jars of pennies. Not everyday pennies, mind you—wheat pennies, the kind that can bring several dollars per coin in today's market. I figured that of all his coins, he wouldn't miss the pennies. I'm sure the clerk at the pharmacy was a little suspicious when I dumped a jarful of wheat pennies on the counter. He took them, though, and I got my water rocket.

I don't remember how my crime was discovered, but I do recall my parents' reaction. They talked with me about what I had done and made me pay my brother back. I remember sitting by my mother and father, waiting for the bad news and assuming that I would be spanked or lose privileges. Instead, they offered mercy. Why? Because they loved me.

Clearly, mercy is a divine quality. We see it in the sacrifice of Jesus Christ for each of us. If we are made in God's image (Gen 1:27), we share His ability to show mercy and other qualities of God. The problem is that mercy, along with forgiveness or grace, doesn't come easily to us. Our humanity gets in the way. Sure, we can and do occasionally offer mercy, but it certainly does not define us.

When we find ourselves at the crucible of either offering or denying mercy, what do humans typically do? Our nature is to go for the throat. I don't know how many times I've sat through a movie where the good guy took relentless abuse only to rise and unleash his fury. What have I done in those instances? I've cheered—literally clapped and yelled.

Real life isn't much different. I've agreed with judgment doled out to offenders with little regard for how, where, or why missteps occurred. Probably more despicably, thoughts have crossed my mind that people who are less fortunate than I deserved their fates, be it the lack of positive relationships, money, or healthcare—you name it. I've thought, "They have screwed up and are getting what they deserve." If you're honest, you have to admit to these actions and thoughts as well. Mercy is not a surface response—it is buried deep within us—we have to work at it to respond in mercy rather than respond in kind.

It's good that we have the potential to be merciful, that we share this quality with God, though it's often undeveloped if not resisted outright. Maybe potential can be a starting point. Maybe being more merciful can be a work in progress.

Learning Mercy

I've proposed that grace is rooted in love and that mercy is a deliberate act of grace when more punitive options are available. If this is the case, having a grace-filled orientation should help us offer mercy when opportunities arise. In Chapter 8, I spoke of ways to increase love in an attempt to allow grace to flourish. How do we become more merciful?

Offering mercy seems tied to an intentional calm. We've already said that when someone offends us, we typically respond in kind. In that moment of anger, frustration, or passion, we too often defer to our darker side. If, however, we maintain an intentional grace-filled calm, the offering of mercy becomes more likely. Even in the heat of the moment, we can weigh alternatives and act in a manner consistent with our core beliefs.

For Christians, that intentional calm is rooted in God. Recently I've found comfort in the thought that "God's got this." I firmly believe it's true on all accounts—God's got this. We sometimes forget that we are in relationship with *the* Creator. If that doesn't give you assurance, what can? The more we engage with Him, the more we recognize His hand in our lives. The more we see His hand, the calmer we can become. A "God's got this" attitude goes a long way toward living a grace-filled life that prepares us to be merciful.

Even in our calm, however, there will be crisis. Flashpoints arise in our lives where, in an instant, we are faced with being merciful or defaulting to other options. What should tip us toward mercy? A couple of things come to mind. As Christians we have received God's mercy through His plan of salvation. We've been there and felt that foot removed from our neck. Appreciation for mercy we have received should strongly influence our own decision to be merciful. In addition, for me, judgment, anger, and revenge are tempered when I remember that every single person is a creation of God. Even that person I'm so eager to condemn shares God's likeness. The image of God is in there somewhere, even if it's not apparent to me. This simple realization of God in others makes it easier to be merciful.

I've seen many baseball games in which a particular batter and pitcher have a history. They've met before and something bad has happened—possibly a homerun followed by the batter's taunt or the pitcher's intentional throw of a brush back pitch (a pitch thrown close to the batter). Both players have a decision to make during their next encounter. Will they move on with the game, or retaliate?

Christians have a decision to make as well. Will we reflect Christ's likeness at every opportunity? Will we show His mercy? Frankly, I'm glad life's a journey. I've got work to do.

Jesus' Teachings About Mercy

You've heard my thoughts about learning mercy, but thank goodness you don't have to rely on me alone! There is so much more to learn from Christ—from His teachings and His life. Two stories come to mind.

In Luke 18:10–14 we learn of two men praying in the temple. One, a Pharisee, stood alone and prayed where he could be heard by others. "God, I thank you that I am not like other people—robbers, evildoers, adulterers—or even like this tax collector. I fast twice a week and give a tenth of all I get." The other man, the tax collector, stood to the side, looked downward, and beat his chest while praying, "God have mercy on me a sinner." In verse 11, Jesus says simply that the tax collector "went home justified before God."

Is there something new here? While the Pharisee did not recognize his need for mercy, the tax collector presented himself humbly and honestly. Does this say that mercy should be restricted only to those who recognize their need for it? I don't think so. I believe mercy was a possibility for both men. What, then, is our takeaway?

I began this chapter by saying that mercy is something we receive and give, though I have primarily focused on our ability to be merciful toward others. This said, I've suggested that one thing allowing us to offer mercy is the realization that we need it too—that we have received God's mercy through His plan of salvation.

The Pharisee did not see his own need for God's mercy. Accordingly, his ability to be merciful toward others could not be informed by personal experience. When faced with his next opportunity to condemn or be merciful, he may well be less likely to respond with mercy. On the other hand, the tax collector knew where he stood with God as he prayed—a sinner in need of redemption. His receipt of God's mercy (after all, he went home justified) creates a foundation from which he can be merciful to others.

Maybe our lesson is one of humility and honesty. Even though, as Christians, we already received God's forgiveness and grace when we accepted Christ, it's not a one-time thing. Throughout our faith journeys we fail, are forgiven, and enjoy grace and mercy. Remember the concept of cheap grace? We must guard against cheapening the entire process of reconciliation with God. Though we participate in this process repeatedly, we must approach it with humility and honesty each time. Like the tax collector, we must realize our need for redemption. From this perspective, we will come to a new appreciation of His mercy that will indeed make us more merciful.

What about learning from a merciful action of Jesus? There are plenty of examples, but one stands out—the woman caught in adultery (John 8:3–11). It was early morning, and Jesus had returned to the temple to teach. A crowd had gathered as the teachers of the law, and the Pharisees appeared with an adulterous woman. Her accusers made her stand before the crowd and then said to Jesus, "Teacher, this woman was caught in the act of adultery. In the law, Moses commanded us to stone such women. Now what do you say?"

There is a lot to unpack here. First, I have to wonder why the woman's accusers left her partner out of this encounter. We can only assume the patriarchal society of the day supported the idea that she carried the primary blame. I bring this up to point out that the woman in question was truly at the bottom of society's barrel. Interestingly, we often find Jesus caring for such people.

I can only imagine the perspectives of all involved. The crowd was likely stunned and maybe a little embarrassed. They knew the law and the peril it posed for the woman. Some might have breathed a sigh of relief, thinking, "Whew, this could have been me last week." Still others probably got a little excited at the prospect of violent justice. Whatever perspective those in the crowd held, we can be assured they were at the edge of their seats with anticipation.

What about the woman? Was she feeling embarrassment, fear, misfortune? My guess is that a host of emotions swirled in her mind as she stood before the crowd, her accusers, and Jesus.

And Jesus, what were His thoughts? Maybe a little bit of "Here we go again." He knew the hearts of everyone in the crowd. I also believe He knew the seriousness of the moment and the weight His response would carry. Jesus had the opportunity to add His foot to the woman's neck—to make her an example—to follow the letter of God's law. Remember I've said that we all have times in which we're at the center of a decision to offer mercy or not. Jesus was there. What did He do?

He bent down and started writing on the ground with His finger. The hand that formed creation took time to make a doodle. Why? I believe Jesus was interjecting a moment of calm assurance into a hot situation. In that instance, I think every person in the that crowd took their eyes off the woman to look at His writing. What did it say? We can only imagine. The point is, it got everyone's attention. It introduced focus and calm into an otherwise uncomfortable event.

We know what happened next. The questions continued and Jesus rose to respond, saying, "Let any one of you who is without sin be the first to throw a stone at her." In our entire lifetimes, few of us will utter such a powerful line. He knelt and began to write once more. One by one, stones dropped and accusers departed. When they had all left, Jesus simply asked, "Woman, where are they? Has no one condemned you?" And she replied, "No one, sir," to which He said, "Then neither do I condemn you, go and leave your life of sin."

The second half of this book has been about learning the qualities of Jesus in an effort to follow Him. The story of the adulterous woman is nothing but a call to a life of offering mercy to others. I think we can take this a step further and say that mercy should be more than a reactive response. It should be our preemptive stance. As we see others condemning, we have an obligation to step into the fray with a merciful alternative. Bryan Stevenson, a Christian lawyer and author, compels us to be preemptively merciful: "Today, our self-righteousness, our fear, and our anger have caused even the Christians to hurl stones at the people who fall down, even when we know we should forgive or show compassion . . . we can't simply watch that happen . . . we have to be stonecatchers."[1]

How many stones have you caught lately? Too often I don't even try. Again, I'm a work in progress.

A FINAL LOOK AT OUR PITCHES

Our metaphorical glove is now full. We have our ongoing recognition of the need to change, God's elegant plan of forgiveness, His love and grace, and now, His mercy. I've presented these ideas in somewhat of a linear fashion. That is, a God-inspired epiphany motivating change leads us to ask for and offer forgiveness, which is made easier by embracing His love and grace. In this chapter, I've suggested that mercy is both a grace-driven action offered at flashpoints where other alternatives are available and a preemptive stance we must take in response to the presence of condemnation all around us.

At this point, it's worth reminding you that I'm not a theologian. I can accept that my ideas may be too simple for some, and I have no intellectual points to make or defend. Why have I focused on God's love, forgiveness, grace, and mercy? Why have I offered these as qualities worth imitating?

Today too many Christians live defeated lives. They either try to do "Jesus stuff" without embracing the power of His message, or they find themselves, like the apostle Paul (Rom 7:14–20), frustrated with their inability to live up to His standard. The Christian life is not about futility—trying to do good, failing, and becoming frustrated with ourselves and others. Instead, it's a process of ongoing transformation. God wants us to be in a constant state of change, to be ever-moving toward His likeness. Each failure is only a momentary setback.

As Christians, we should live each day with eager anticipation of "being Jesus" to the next person on our paths and the absolute confidence that God's love, forgiveness, grace, and mercy are always there to get us back on track when we falter. Our transformation to His likeness will be challenging at times, but what worth pursuing in this life isn't?

I presented mercy as my final pitch because I believe it develops with Christian maturity. Being merciful in the moment requires a calm assurance that doesn't come naturally. Likewise, preemptively offering mercy

1. Bryan Stevenson, *Just Mercy: A Story of Justice and Redemption* (New York: Spiegel and Grau, 2014), 309.

requires courage. These attributes characterize the life of Jesus and the "all in" Christian dedicated to His service.

POTENTIAL IMPACT OF MERCY ON MEAN CHRISTIANITY

Mercy is a game-changer. It has the ability to take away life's sting. As an alternative pitch to judgment, mercy puts us actively in the field rather than behind the plate. If pursued in a costly manner, it is nothing if not transformative.

Offering mercy at the flashpoints in our lives calls us to live with a calm assurance. In contrast, a preemptive inclination to offer mercy (to be a stonecatcher) puts us actively intervening in condemnation around us— averting flashpoints before they start or, in the midst of judgment, encouraging others to consider alternatives to what they perceive as "deserved" outcomes.

Let's first look at the potential impact of flashpoint mercy on mean Christianity. In Chapter 3, I provided examples of mean Christianity from both the corporate body of Christ and from individual actions. Remember the "other people" corporate example of mean Christianity, the tendency to see others as different or undeserving due to their gender, race, religion, sexual orientation, or for some other reason? Assume you are in a fellowship where an "other people" issue suddenly arises that could alter who is allowed to worship with you. There is a flood of emotion and the potential for visceral reactions is high. In this instance, your corporate body is at a flashpoint. For whatever reason or prejudice, they are judging and offering what they see as a deserved fate: Exclusion.

This situation could become quite heated. Remarks could be divisive, and a negative outcome may diminish the church's broader impact in the community. As the interaction reaches a fever pitch, could you be the one to metaphorically kneel and write in the dirt? Could you interject calm while reminding others of Jesus' example of inclusiveness? Could you suggest a merciful alternative?

This example illustrates how collective flashpoints within the body of Christ easily provide opportunities for either meanness or mercy. Pausing reflectively and offering a calm voice can go a long way toward the generation of a Christlike solution.

I know the situation described above could as easily lead to continued conflict as to resolution. That is not your worry. Your concern is being Jesus in the example. Let God manage it from there.

Flashpoint mercy opportunities for individual Christians come every day in our interactions with others. Take social media as an example. I've shared how easy it is for us to be mean when behind the anonymity of a screen. We see something that gets under our skin and rush to respond. We judge what we read, and we want our say.

What if we offered mercy? What if the next time we read something that really deserved a searing response, we simply offered an expression of God's love? It might spur additional meanness, but it could also provoke positive reflection.

Let's move our discussion to preemptive mercy. How could an ongoing readiness to offer mercy impact mean Christianity? If Christians lived lives characterized by preemptive mercy, meanness would be history.

A Christian struggling with meanness is likely judging others. Their judgment may be based in what they perceive to be biblical truths. So, in their minds, their meanness is justified. But remember the dangers of righteous indignation—simply put, this path is a slippery slope.

If we interject preemptive mercy into the life of the mean Christian, judgment is replaced by mercy. Individuals can continue to hold their opinions specific to the "Bible truth" informing their judgment, yet offer mercy in the place of that judgment. Beliefs related to sexual orientation or gender roles provide clear examples of this possibility. Christians often cling to exclusionary opinions in these areas that they feel are rooted in scripture. I'm not saying this isn't their right. Remember, I believe we have the unique and individual privilege of interpreting God's word as He leads us by His Spirit. What I am suggesting is that regardless of our opinions, the option of offering mercy is always there. Someone in disagreement with homosexuality can, then, through a preemptive act of mercy, welcome a homosexual into their worship fellowship. Likewise, a person who disagrees with women in leadership roles in the church can, through a preemptive act of mercy, hear and learn from a woman sharing God's word.

Preemptive mercy is a lifestyle of "merciful readiness." It is not only stonecatching as we observe others condemning, it is clearing the path of stones before condemnation takes root. How many times in a day could each of us defuse condemnation with a deft insertion of kindness? Face it, stones are all around us, and there is much work to do.

I recently shared my ideas about flashpoint and preemptive mercy with a Christian friend. Her comment was real and to the point. She said, "Bill, what you are saying is hard to live." My friend is right, and I openly admit to failing to offer mercy each day. That said, there is hope. Remember theme 5 from Chapter 2 says, "Jesus sets a high bar for living."

My wife recently directed me to a *Sojourners* article about grace and mercy.[2] The article told the story of former neo-Nazis in America, with an emphasis on how these individuals had found their way from hatred to an orientation of love and inclusion. One man's journey began at McDonald's. As he handed money to an elderly woman of color, she noticed a swastika on his hand and kindly said, "Oh honey, you are so much better than that." The recognition of his potential for good, from a person representing those he had so often condemned, lit a flame of change in his life.

Change begins one encounter at a time. One offer of mercy can plant the seed for so many others. Are you willing to try? I bet there are stones all around you. Time to get busy.

2. Jason Byassee, "Confessions of a Former White Supremacist," *Sojourners*, August 2017.

CHAPTER 10

A New Life in Christ

D o you know what I appreciate the most about being a Christian? The fact that each moment, hour, and day is new in Christ. I don't ever have to look back on my failures. They are forgiven and forgotten. My ongoing and lifelong process of reconciliation with God has me constantly on a new, fresh path. A path leading to His likeness.

This book has presented Christian meanness as a problem for the faith that not only damages the brand of Christianity but keeps others from knowing its benefits. What's the good news? There is a solution: Reconciliation with our God. We can ask for and receive God's forgiveness, accept and live within His love and grace, and extend His mercy the next time around. We're not doomed to defeat. To the contrary, we are poised for victory. I'm not saying this is easy; I'm saying it's possible.

What's the key? Simply, living like Jesus. Every moment, every day, being Jesus to the person in front of you. Living your life in a way consistent with the themes that characterized His life. In Chapter 2, I described this as following His call to caring and responding; to authenticity; to the values of selflessness, humility, love, compassion, kindness, and faith; to an aspirational "high bar" life; and to righteous indignation in response to this world's unfairness.

Allow me one final baseball metaphor. Imagine you're a baseball player, and it's the first game of a new season. Last year's record is a distant memory. It just doesn't matter. You arrive at the park early to take in every aspect of the game. The sky is crystal clear, and a light wind blows the flags at the top of the stadium. Vendors are preparing their wares—popcorn is popping, and products are being stocked for the coming crowd.

The equipment bag over your shoulder feels lighter today. In fact, your gear seems weightless. A new season brings a quicker step, new possibilities. Anything can happen.

You pause a moment before entering the clubhouse to take a glance back at the arriving crowd. Families are laughing. Everyone is radiant with unabashed hopefulness. Once with your team, you dress and go over final preparations. The coach shares a few thoughts about keeping focused on what is important, about all those repetitions of training camp.

You rise with your teammates to take the field. Shoulder to shoulder, you exit the clubhouse down a long, dark corridor leading to the field. All you hear are the clicks and clacks of cleats on concrete. At the end of the corridor, brightness overwhelms the dark as the team spills on to the diamond.

Emotions run high as players warm up to grandstand music and cheers from the crowd. It's finally game time. The coach singles you out for a few words. He reminds you that you're prepared, that you've got all the throws. Putting the ball in your glove, he smiles at you confidently. You walk slowly to the mound for a few pitches. The first batter steps up to the plate. The umpire yells "Play ball."

This story is about the present—your present as a Christian. At this very moment, you have the potential to start a new season, a new life in Christ. The past is irrelevant. Possibilities for you both as an individual and as a member of the body of Christ have never been better. If meanness has characterized your life, it doesn't have to continue. If the meanness of others has dogged you every step of every day, it can stop. Reconciliation and the joys of an "all in" life are there for you. At this very moment, things can change.

The next step is yours alone. What's my advice? Play your position.

NIV Bible Verses Used Provided Alphabetically

Acts 7:54–60 [54] When the members of the Sanhedrin heard this, they were furious and gnashed their teeth at him. [55] But Stephen, full of the Holy Spirit, looked up to heaven and saw the glory of God, and Jesus standing at the right hand of God. [56] "Look," he said, "I see heaven open and the Son of Man standing at the right hand of God." [57] At this they covered their ears and, yelling at the top of their voices, they all rushed at him, [58] dragged him out of the city and began to stone him. Meanwhile, the witnesses laid their coats at the feet of a young man named Saul. [59] While they were stoning him, Stephen prayed, "Lord Jesus, receive my spirit." [60] Then he fell on his knees and cried out, "Lord, do not hold this sin against them." When he had said this, he fell asleep.

Acts 10:9–16 [9] About noon the following day as they were on their journey and approaching the city, Peter went up on the roof to pray. [10] He became hungry and wanted something to eat, and while the meal was being prepared, he fell into a trance. [11] He saw heaven opened and something like a large sheet being let down to earth by its four corners. [12] It contained all kinds of four-footed animals, as well as reptiles and birds. [13] Then a voice told him, "Get up, Peter. Kill and eat." [14] "Surely not, Lord!" Peter replied. "I have never eaten anything impure or unclean." [15] The voice spoke to him a second time, "Do not call anything impure that God has made clean."

[16] This happened three times, and immediately the sheet was taken back to heaven.

Act 15:36–41 [36] Some time later Paul said to Barnabas, "Let us go back and visit the believers in all the towns where we preached the word of the Lord and see how they are doing." [37] Barnabas wanted to take John, also called Mark, with them, [38] but Paul did not think it wise to take him, because he had deserted them in Pamphylia and had not continued with them in the work. [39] They had such a sharp disagreement that they parted company. Barnabas took Mark and sailed for Cyprus, [40] but Paul chose Silas and left, commended by the believers to the grace of the Lord. [41] He went through Syria and Cilicia, strengthening the churches.

Acts 26:20 First to those in Damascus, then to those in Jerusalem and in all Judea, and then to the Gentiles, I preached that they should repent and turn to God and demonstrate their repentance by their deeds.

Daniel 7:13 In my vision at night I looked, and there before me was one like a son of man, coming with the clouds of heaven. He approached the Ancient of Days and was led into his presence. [14] He was given authority, glory and sovereign power; all nations and peoples of every language worshiped him. His dominion is an everlasting dominion that will not pass away, and his kingdom is one that will never be destroyed.

Galatians 2:6–10 [6] As for those who were held in high esteem—whatever they were makes no difference to me; God does not show favoritism—they added nothing to my message. [7] On the contrary, they recognized that I had been entrusted with the task of preaching the gospel to the uncircumcised, just as Peter had been to the circumcised. [8] For God, who was at work in Peter as an apostle to the circumcised, was also at work in me as an apostle to the Gentiles. [9] James, Cephas and John, those esteemed as pillars, gave me and Barnabas the right hand of fellowship when they recognized the grace given to me. They agreed that we should go to the Gentiles, and they to the circumcised. [10] All they asked was that we should continue to remember the poor, the very thing I had been eager to do all along.

Genesis 1:27 So God created man in his own image, in the image of God he created him; male and female he created them.

James 2:1–7 My brothers and sisters, believers in our glorious Lord Jesus Christ must not show favoritism. ² Suppose a man comes into your meeting wearing a gold ring and fine clothes, and a poor man in filthy old clothes also comes in. ³ If you show special attention to the man wearing fine clothes and say, "Here's a good seat for you," but say to the poor man, "You stand there" or "Sit on the floor by my feet," ⁴ have you not discriminated among yourselves and become judges with evil thoughts? ⁵ Listen, my dear brothers and sisters: Has not God chosen those who are poor in the eyes of the world to be rich in faith and to inherit the kingdom he promised those who love him? ⁶ But you have dishonored the poor. Is it not the rich who are exploiting you? Are they not the ones who are dragging you into court? ⁷ Are they not the ones who are blaspheming the noble name of him to whom you belong?

James 3:5–6 ⁵Likewise, the tongue is a small part of the body, but it makes great boasts. Consider what a great forest is set on fire by a small spark. ⁶ The tongue also is a fire, a world of evil among the parts of the body. It corrupts the whole body, sets the whole course of one's life on fire, and is itself set on fire by hell.

John 2:7–10 ⁷ Jesus said to the servants, "Fill the jars with water." And they filled them up to the brim. ⁸ And he said to them, "Now draw some out and take it to the master of the feast." So they took it. ⁹ When the master of the feast tasted the water now become wine, and did not know where it came from (though the servants who had drawn the water knew), the master of the feast called the bridegroom ¹⁰ and said to him, "Everyone serves the good wine first, and when people have drunk freely, then the poor wine. But you have kept the good wine until now."

John 2:15 So he made a whip out of cords, and drove all from the temple courts, both sheep and cattle; he scattered the coins of the money changers and overturned their tables.

John 4:7–15 ⁷ When a Samaritan woman came to draw water, Jesus said to her, "Will you give me a drink?" ⁸ (His disciples had gone into the town to buy food.) ⁹ The Samaritan woman said to him, "You are a Jew and I am a Samaritan woman. How can you ask me for a drink?" (For Jews do not associate with Samaritans.) ¹⁰ Jesus answered her, "If you knew the gift of God and who it is that asks you for a drink, you would have asked him and he would have given you living water." ¹¹ "Sir," the woman said, "you have nothing to draw with and the well is deep. Where can you get this living water? [12] Are you greater than our father Jacob, who gave us the well and drank from it himself, as did also his sons and his livestock?" [13] Jesus answered, "Everyone who drinks this water will be thirsty again, [14] but whoever drinks the water I give them will never thirst. Indeed, the water I give them will become in them a spring of water welling up to eternal life." [15] The woman said to him, "Sir, give me this water so that I won't get thirsty and have to keep coming here to draw water."

John 5:6–11 [6] When Jesus saw him lying there and learned that he had been in this condition for a long time, he asked him, "Do you want to get well?" [7] "Sir," the invalid replied, "I have no one to help me into the pool when the water is stirred. While I am trying to get in, someone else goes down ahead of me." [8] Then Jesus said to him, "Get up! Pick up your mat and walk." [9] At once the man was cured; he picked up his mat and walked. The day on which this took place was a Sabbath, [10] and so the Jewish leaders said to the man who had been healed, "It is the Sabbath; the law forbids you to carry your mat." [11] But he replied, "The man who made me well said to me, 'Pick up your mat and walk.' "

John 8:3–11 [3] The teachers of the law and the Pharisees brought in a woman caught in adultery. They made her stand before the group [4] and said to Jesus, "Teacher, this woman was caught in the act of adultery. [5] In the Law Moses commanded us to stone such women. Now what do you say?" [6] They were using this question as a trap, in order to have a basis for accusing him.

But Jesus bent down and started to write on the ground with his finger. [7] When they kept on questioning him, he straightened up and said to them, "Let any one of you who is without sin be the first to throw a stone at her." [8] Again he stooped down and wrote on the ground.

[9] At this, those who heard began to go away one at a time, the older ones first, until only Jesus was left, with the woman still standing there. [10] Jesus straightened up and asked her, "Woman, where are they? Has no one condemned you?" [11] "No one, sir," she said. "Then neither do I condemn you," Jesus declared. "Go now and leave your life of sin."

John 9:6–7 [6] Having said these things, he spit on the ground and made mud with the saliva. Then he anointed the man's eyes with the mud [7] and said to him, "Go, wash in the pool of Siloam" (which means Sent). So he went and washed and came back seeing.

John 11:35 Jesus wept.

John 11:38–44 [38] Then Jesus, deeply moved again, came to the tomb. It was a cave, and a stone lay against it. [39] Jesus said, "Take away the stone." Martha, the sister of the dead man, said to him, "Lord, by this time there will be an odor, for he has been dead four days." [40] Jesus said to her, "Did I not tell you that if you believed you would see the glory of God?" [41] So they took away the stone. And Jesus lifted up his eyes and said, "Father, I thank you that you have heard me. [42] I knew that you always hear me, but I said this on account of the people standing around, that they may believe that you sent me." [43] When he had said these things, he cried out with a loud voice, "Lazarus, come out." [44] The man who had died came out, his hands and feet bound with linen strips, and his face wrapped with a cloth. Jesus said to them, "Unbind him, and let him go."

John 15:13 Greater love has no one than this: to lay down one's life for one's friends.

John 20:11–14 [11] Now Mary stood outside the tomb crying. As she wept, she bent over to look into the tomb [12] and saw two angels in white, seated where Jesus' body had been, one at the head and the other at the foot. [13] They asked her, "Woman, why are you crying?" "They have taken my Lord away," she said, "and I don't know where they have put him." [14] At this, she turned around and saw Jesus standing there, but she did not realize that it was Jesus.

John 21:6 He said, "Throw your net on the right side of the boat and you will find some." When they did, they were unable to haul the net in because of the large number of fish.

Luke 2:40 And the child grew and became strong; he was filled with wisdom, and the grace of God was on him.

Luke 4:35 "Be quiet!" Jesus said sternly. "Come out of him!" Then the demon threw the man down before them all and came out without injuring him.

Luke 6:27–28 [27] "But to you who are listening I say: Love your enemies, do good to those who hate you, [28] bless those who curse you, pray for those who mistreat you.

Luke 7:6–10 [6] So Jesus went with them. He was not far from the house when the centurion sent friends to say to him: "Lord, don't trouble yourself, for I do not deserve to have you come under my roof. [7] That is why I did not even consider myself worthy to come to you. But say the word, and my servant will be healed. [8] For I myself am a man under authority, with soldiers under me. I tell this one, 'Go,' and he goes; and that one, 'Come,' and he comes. I say to my servant, 'Do this,' and he does it." [9] When Jesus heard this, he was amazed at him, and turning to the crowd following him, he said, "I tell you, I have not found such great faith even in Israel." [10] Then the men who had been sent returned to the house and found the servant well.

Luke 7:11–17 [11] Soon afterward, Jesus went to a town called Nain, and his disciples and a large crowd went along with him. [12] As he approached the town gate, a dead person was being carried out—the only son of his mother, and she was a widow. And a large crowd from the town was with her. [13] When the Lord saw her, his heart went out to her and he said, "Don't cry."

[14] Then he went up and touched the bier they were carrying him on, and the bearers stood still. He said, "Young man, I say to you, get up!" [15] The dead man sat up and began to talk, and Jesus gave him back to his mother. [16] They were all filled with awe and praised God. "A great prophet has appeared among us," they said. "God has come to help his people." [17] This news about Jesus spread throughout Judea and the surrounding country.

Luke 7: 30–37 [30] In reply Jesus said: "A man was going down from Jerusalem to Jericho, when he was attacked by robbers. They stripped him of his clothes, beat him and went away, leaving him half dead. [31] A priest happened to be going down the same road, and when he saw the man, he passed by on the other side. [32] So too, a Levite, when he came to the place and saw him, passed by on the other side. [33] But a Samaritan, as he traveled, came where the man was; and when he saw him, he took pity on him. [34] He went to him and bandaged his wounds, pouring on oil and wine. Then he put the man on his own donkey, brought him to an inn and took care of him. [35] The next day he took out two denarii[c] and gave them to the innkeeper. 'Look after him,' he said, 'and when I return, I will reimburse you for any extra expense you may have.'

[36] "Which of these three do you think was a neighbor to the man who fell into the hands of robbers?" [37] The expert in the law replied, "The one who had mercy on him."

Luke 8:43–44 [43] And a woman was there who had been subject to bleeding for twelve years,[a] but no one could heal her. [44] She came up behind him and touched the edge of his cloak, and immediately her bleeding stopped.

Luke 9:37–41 [37] The next day, when they came down from the mountain, a large crowd met him. [38] A man in the crowd called out, "Teacher, I beg you to look at my son, for he is my only child. [39] A spirit seizes him and he suddenly screams; it throws him into convulsions so that he foams at the mouth. It scarcely ever leaves him and is destroying him. [40] I begged your disciples to drive it out, but they could not." [41] "You unbelieving and perverse generation," Jesus replied, "how long shall I stay with you and put up with you? Bring your son here."

Luke 10:29–36 [29] But he, desiring to justify himself, said to Jesus, "And who is my neighbor?" [30] Jesus replied, "A man was going down from Jerusalem to Jericho, and he fell among robbers, who stripped him and beat him and departed, leaving him half dead. [31] Now by chance a priest was going down that road, and when he saw him he passed by on the other side. [32] So likewise a Levite, when he came to the place and saw him, passed by on the other side. [33] But a Samaritan, as he journeyed, came to where he was, and when he saw him, he had compassion. [34] He went to him and bound up his wounds, pouring on oil and wine. Then he set him on his own animal and brought him to an inn and took care of him. [35] And the next day he took out two denarii[a] and gave them to the innkeeper, saying, 'Take care of him, and whatever more you spend, I will repay you when I come back.' [36] Which of these three, do you think, proved to be a neighbor to the man who fell among the robbers?"

Luke 10:38–42 [38] As Jesus and his disciples were on their way, he came to a village where a woman named Martha opened her home to him. [39] She had a sister called Mary, who sat at the Lord's feet listening to what he said. [40] But Martha was distracted by all the preparations that had to be made. She came to him and asked, "Lord, don't you care that my sister has left me to do the work by myself? Tell her to help me!" [41] "Martha, Martha," the Lord answered, "you are worried and upset about many things, [42] but few things are needed—or indeed only one. Mary has chosen what is better, and it will not be taken away from her."

Luke 12:15 Then he said to them, "Watch out! Be on your guard against all kinds of greed; life does not consist in an abundance of possessions."

Luke 15:1–10 Now the tax collectors and sinners were all gathering around to hear Jesus. ² But the Pharisees and the teachers of the law muttered, "This man welcomes sinners and eats with them." ³ Then Jesus told them this parable: ⁴ "Suppose one of you has a hundred sheep and loses one of them. Doesn't he leave the ninety-nine in the open country and go after the lost sheep until he finds it? ⁵ And when he finds it, he joyfully puts it on his shoulders ⁶ and goes home. Then he calls his friends and neighbors together and says, 'Rejoice with me; I have found my lost sheep.' ⁷ I tell you that in the same way there will be more rejoicing in heaven over one sinner who repents than over ninety-nine righteous persons who do not need to repent. ⁸ "Or suppose a woman has ten silver coins and loses one. Doesn't she light a lamp, sweep the house and search carefully until she finds it? ⁹ And when she finds it, she calls her friends and neighbors together and says, 'Rejoice with me; I have found my lost coin.' ¹⁰ In the same way, I tell you, there is rejoicing in the presence of the angels of God over one sinner who repents."

Luke 15:17–24 ¹⁷ "When he came to his senses, he said, 'How many of my father's hired servants have food to spare, and here I am starving to death! ¹⁸ I will set out and go back to my father and say to him: Father, I have sinned against heaven and against you. ¹⁹ I am no longer worthy to be called your son; make me like one of your hired servants.' ²⁰ So he got up and went to his father. "But while he was still a long way off, his father saw him and was filled with compassion for him; he ran to his son, threw his arms around him and kissed him.

²¹ "The son said to him, 'Father, I have sinned against heaven and against you. I am no longer worthy to be called your son.' ²² "But the father said to his servants, 'Quick! Bring the best robe and put it on him. Put a ring on his finger and sandals on his feet. ²³ Bring the fattened calf and kill it. Let's have a feast and celebrate. ²⁴ For this son of mine was dead and is alive again; he was lost and is found.' So they began to celebrate.

Luke 17:2 It would be better for them to be thrown into the sea with a millstone tied around their neck than to cause one of these little ones to stumble.

Luke 17:6 He replied, "If you have faith as small as a mustard seed, you can say to this mulberry tree, 'Be uprooted and planted in the sea,' and it will obey you.

Luke 18:10–14 "Two men went up to the temple to pray, one a Pharisee and the other a tax collector. [11] The Pharisee stood by himself and prayed: 'God, I thank you that I am not like other people—robbers, evildoers, adulterers—or even like this tax collector. [12] I fast twice a week and give a tenth of all I get.' [13] "But the tax collector stood at a distance. He would not even look up to heaven, but beat his breast and said, 'God, have mercy on me, a sinner.' [14] "I tell you that this man, rather than the other, went home justified before God. For all those who exalt themselves will be humbled, and those who humble themselves will be exalted."

Luke 22:42 "Father, if you are willing, take this cup from me; yet not my will, but yours be done."

Luke 24:2–7 [2] They found the stone rolled away from the tomb, [3] but when they entered, they did not find the body of the Lord Jesus. [4] While they were wondering about this, suddenly two men in clothes that gleamed like lightning stood beside them. [5] In their fright the women bowed down with their faces to the ground, but the men said to them, "Why do you look for the living among the dead? [6] He is not here; he has risen! Remember how he told you, while he was still with you in Galilee: [7] 'The Son of Man must be delivered over to the hands of sinners, be crucified and on the third day be raised again.' "

Luke 24:13–24 [13] Now that same day two of them were going to a village called Emmaus, about seven miles from Jerusalem. [14] They were talking with each other about everything that had happened. [15] As they talked and discussed these things with each other, Jesus himself came up and walked along with them; [16] but they were kept from recognizing him. [17] He asked them, "What are you discussing together as you walk along?" They stood still, their faces downcast. [18] One of them, named Cleopas, asked him, "Are you the only one visiting Jerusalem who does not know the things that have happened there in these days?" [19] "What things?" he asked. "About Jesus of Nazareth," they replied. "He was a prophet, powerful in word and deed before God and all the people. [20] The chief priests and our rulers handed him over to be sentenced to death, and they crucified him; [21] but we had hoped that he was the one who was going to redeem Israel. And what is more, it is the third day since all this took place. [22] In addition, some of our women amazed us. They went to the tomb early this morning [23] but didn't find his body. They came and told us that they had seen a vision of angels, who said he was alive. [24] Then some of our companions went to the tomb and found it just as the women had said, but they did not see Jesus."

Mark 1:25 [25] "Be quiet!" said Jesus sternly. "Come out of him!"

Mark 1:40–42 A man suffering from a dreaded skin disease came to Jesus, knelt down, and begged him for help. "If you want to," he said, "you can make me clean." [41] Jesus was filled with pity, and reached out and touched him. "I do want to," he answered. "Be clean!" [42] At once the disease left the man, and he was clean.

Mark 2:11–12 [11] "I say to you, rise, pick up your bed, and go home." [12] And he rose and immediately picked up his bed and went out before them all, so that they were all amazed and glorified God, saying, "We never saw anything like this!"

Mark 2:23–27 [23] One Sabbath Jesus was going through the grainfields, and as his disciples walked along, they began to pick some heads of grain. [24] The Pharisees said to him, "Look, why are they doing what is unlawful on the Sabbath?" [25] He answered, "Have you never read what David did when he and his companions were hungry and in need? [26] In the days of Abiathar the high priest, he entered the house of God and ate the consecrated bread, which is lawful only for priests to eat. And he also gave some to his companions." [27] Then he said to them, "The Sabbath was made for man, not man for the Sabbath.

Mark 3:5 [3] Jesus said to the man with the shriveled hand, "Stand up in front of everyone."

[4] Then Jesus asked them, "Which is lawful on the Sabbath: to do good or to do evil, to save life or to kill?" But they remained silent. [5] He looked around at them in anger and, deeply distressed at their stubborn hearts, said to the man, "Stretch out your hand." He stretched it out, and his hand was completely restored.

Mark 4:35–41 [35] That day when evening came, he said to his disciples, "Let us go over to the other side." [36] Leaving the crowd behind, they took him along, just as he was, in the boat. There were also other boats with him. [37] A furious squall came up, and the waves broke over the boat, so that it was nearly swamped. [38] Jesus was in the stern, sleeping on a cushion. The disciples woke him and said to him, "Teacher, don't you care if we drown?"

[39] He got up, rebuked the wind and said to the waves, "Quiet! Be still!" Then the wind died down and it was completely calm. [40] He said to his disciples, "Why are you so afraid? Do you still have no faith?" [41] They were terrified and asked each other, "Who is this? Even the wind and the waves obey him!"

Mark 5:34 He said to her, "Daughter, your faith has healed you. Go in peace and be freed from your suffering."

Mark 7:1–5 The Pharisees and some of the teachers of the law who had come from Jerusalem gathered around Jesus [2] and saw some of his disciples eating food with hands that were defiled, that is, unwashed. [3] (The Pharisees and all the Jews do not eat unless they give their hands a ceremonial washing, holding to the tradition of the elders. [4] When they come from the marketplace they do not eat unless they wash. And they observe many other traditions, such as the washing of cups, pitchers and kettles.) [5] So the Pharisees and teachers of the law asked Jesus, "Why don't your disciples live according to the tradition of the elders instead of eating their food with defiled hands?"

Mark 7:32–35 [32] And they brought to him a man who was deaf and had a speech impediment, and they begged him to lay his hand on him. [33] And taking him aside from the crowd privately, he put his fingers into his ears, and after spitting touched his tongue. [34] And looking up to heaven, he sighed and said to him, "Ephphatha," that is, "Be opened." [35] And his ears were opened, his tongue was released, and he spoke plainly.

Mark 9:42 If anyone causes one of these little ones—those who believe in me—to stumble, it would be better for them if a large millstone were hung around their neck and they were thrown into the sea.

Mark 10:21–25 [21] Jesus looked at him and loved him. "One thing you lack," he said. "Go, sell everything you have and give to the poor, and you will have treasure in heaven. Then come, follow me." [22] At this the man's face fell. He went away sad, because he had great wealth. [23] Jesus looked around and said to his disciples, "How hard it is for the rich to enter the kingdom of God!" [24] The disciples were amazed at his words. But Jesus said again, "Children, how hard it is to enter the kingdom of God! [25] It is easier for a camel to go through the eye of a needle than for someone who is rich to enter the kingdom of God."

Mark 10:52 "Go," said Jesus, "your faith has healed you." Immediately he received his sight and followed Jesus along the road.

Mark 12:31 The second is this: 'Love your neighbor as yourself.'[a] There is no commandment greater than these."

Mark 16:6–7 ⁶ "Don't be alarmed," he said. "You are looking for Jesus the Nazarene, who was crucified. He has risen! He is not here. See the place where they laid him. ⁷ But go, tell his disciples and Peter, 'He is going ahead of you into Galilee. There you will see him, just as he told you.'"

Matthew 5:21–22; 27–30 ²¹ "You have heard that it was said to the people long ago, 'You shall not murder, and anyone who murders will be subject to judgment.' ²² But I tell you that anyone who is angry with a brother or sister will be subject to judgment. Again, anyone who says to a brother or sister, 'Raca,' is answerable to the court. And anyone who says, 'You fool!' will be in danger of the fire of hell. . . . ²⁷ "You have heard that it was said, 'You shall not commit adultery.' ²⁸ But I tell you that anyone who looks at a woman lustfully has already committed adultery with her in his heart. ²⁹ If your right eye causes you to stumble, gouge it out and throw it away. It is better for you to lose one part of your body than for your whole body to be thrown into hell. ³⁰ And if your right hand causes you to stumble, cut it off and throw it away. It is better for you to lose one part of your body than for your whole body to go into hell.

Matthew 6:25–27 ²⁵ "Therefore I tell you, do not worry about your life, what you will eat or drink; or about your body, what you will wear. Is not life more than food, and the body more than clothes? ²⁶ Look at the birds of the air; they do not sow or reap or store away in barns, and yet your heavenly Father feeds them. Are you not much more valuable than they? ²⁷ Can any one of you by worrying add a single hour to your life?

Matthew 7:1–3 Do not judge, or you too will be judged. ² For in the same way you judge others, you will be judged, and with the measure you use, it will be measured to you. ³ "Why do you look at the speck of sawdust in your brother's eye and pay no attention to the plank in your own eye?

Matthew 8:3 ³ Jesus reached out his hand and touched the man. "I am willing," he said. "Be clean!" Immediately he was cleansed of his leprosy.

Matthew 8:5–13 [5] When Jesus had entered Capernaum, a centurion came to him, asking for help. [6] "Lord," he said, "my servant lies at home paralyzed, suffering terribly." [7] Jesus said to him, "Shall I come and heal him?" [8] The centurion replied, "Lord, I do not deserve to have you come under my roof. But just say the word, and my servant will be healed. [9] For I myself am a man under authority, with soldiers under me. I tell this one, 'Go,' and he goes; and that one, 'Come,' and he comes. I say to my servant, 'Do this,' and he does it." [10] When Jesus heard this, he was amazed and said to those following him, "Truly I tell you, I have not found anyone in Israel with such great faith. [11] I say to you that many will come from the east and the west, and will take their places at the feast with Abraham, Isaac and Jacob in the kingdom of heaven. [12] But the subjects of the kingdom will be thrown outside, into the darkness, where there will be weeping and gnashing of teeth." [13] Then Jesus said to the centurion, "Go! Let it be done just as you believed it would." And his servant was healed at that moment.

Matthew 12:10–11 [10] and a man with a shriveled hand was there. Looking for a reason to bring charges against Jesus, they asked him, "Is it lawful to heal on the Sabbath?" [11] He said to them, "If any of you has a sheep and it falls into a pit on the Sabbath, will you not take hold of it and lift it out?

Matthew 13:15 For this people's heart has become calloused; they hardly hear with their ears, and they have closed their eyes. Otherwise they might see with their eyes, hear with their ears, understand with their hearts and turn, and I would heal them.

Matthew 14:16–21 [16] Jesus replied, "They do not need to go away. You give them something to eat." [17] "We have here only five loaves of bread and two fish," they answered. [18] "Bring them here to me," he said. [19] And he directed the people to sit down on the grass. Taking the five loaves and the two fish and looking up to heaven, he gave thanks and broke the loaves. Then he gave them to the disciples, and the disciples gave them to the people. [20] They all ate and were satisfied, and the disciples picked up twelve basketfuls of broken pieces that were left over. [21] The number of those who ate was about five thousand men, besides women and children.

Matthew 14:22–27 [22] Immediately Jesus made the disciples get into the boat and go on ahead of him to the other side, while he dismissed the crowd. [23] After he had dismissed them, he went up on a mountainside by himself to pray. Later that night, he was there alone, [24] and the boat was already a considerable distance from land, buffeted by the waves because the wind was against it. ²⁵ Shortly before dawn Jesus went out to them, walking on the lake. ²⁶ When the disciples saw him walking on the lake, they were terrified. "It's a ghost," they said, and cried out in fear. ²⁷ But Jesus immediately said to them: "Take courage! It is I. Don't be afraid."

Matthew 15:7 ⁷ You hypocrites! Isaiah was right when he prophesied about you "'These people honor me with their lips, but their hearts are far from me. They worship me in vain.'"

Matthew 15:22–28 ²² A Canaanite woman from that vicinity came to him, crying out, "Lord, Son of David, have mercy on me! My daughter is demon-possessed and suffering terribly."

²³ Jesus did not answer a word. So his disciples came to him and urged him, "Send her away, for she keeps crying out after us." ²⁴ He answered, "I was sent only to the lost sheep of Israel."

²⁵ The woman came and knelt before him. "Lord, help me!" she said. ²⁶ He replied, "It is not right to take the children's bread and toss it to the dogs." ²⁷ "Yes it is, Lord," she said. "Even the dogs eat the crumbs that fall from their master's table." ²⁸ Then Jesus said to her, "Woman, you have great faith! Your request is granted." And her daughter was healed at that moment.

Matthew 18:6 If anyone causes one of these little ones—those who believe in me—to stumble, it would be better for them to have a large millstone hung around their neck and to be drowned in the depths of the sea.

Matthew 18:15–17 ¹⁵ "If your brother or sister sins, go and point out their fault, just between the two of you. If they listen to you, you have won them over. ¹⁶ But if they will not listen, take one or two others along, so that 'every matter may be established by the testimony of two or three witnesses.' ¹⁷ If they still refuse to listen, tell it to the church; and if they refuse to listen even to the church, treat them as you would a pagan or a tax collector.

Matthew 19:14 Jesus said, "Let the little children come to me, and do not hinder them, for the kingdom of heaven belongs to such as these."

Matthew 20:16 "So the last will be first, and the first will be last."

Matthew 21–12-13 ¹² Jesus entered the temple courts and drove out all who were buying and selling there. He overturned the tables of the money changers and the benches of those selling doves. [13] "It is written," he said to them, "'My house will be called a house of prayer,' but you are making it 'a den of robbers.'"

Matthew 22:19–21 [19] Show me the coin used for paying the tax." They brought him a denarius, [20] and he asked them, "Whose image is this? And whose inscription?" [21] "Caesar's," they replied.

Then he said to them, "So give back to Caesar what is Caesar's, and to God what is God's."

Matthew 23:2–7 2 "The teachers of the law and the Pharisees sit in Moses' seat. [3] So you must be careful to do everything they tell you. But do not do what they do, for they do not practice what they preach. [4] They tie up heavy, cumbersome loads and put them on other people's shoulders, but they themselves are not willing to lift a finger to move them. [5] "Everything they do is done for people to see: They make their phylacteries[a] wide and the tassels on their garments long; [6] they love the place of honor at banquets and the most important seats in the synagogues; [7] they love to be greeted with respect in the marketplaces and to be called 'Rabbi' by others.

Matthew 24:24 For false messiahs and false prophets will appear and perform great signs and wonders to deceive, if possible, even the elect.

Matthew 25:40 "The King will reply, 'Truly I tell you, whatever you did for one of the least of these brothers and sisters of mine, you did for me.'

Matthew 26:7–12 [7] a woman came to him with an alabaster jar of very expensive perfume, which she poured on his head as he was reclining at the table. [8] When the disciples saw this, they were indignant. "Why this waste?" they asked. [9] "This perfume could have been sold at a high price and the money given to the poor." [10] Aware of this, Jesus said to them, "Why are you bothering this woman? She has done a beautiful thing to me. [11] The poor you will always have with you, but you will not always have me. [12] When she poured this perfume on my body, she did it to prepare me for burial.

Matthew 28:5–7 [5] The angel said to the women, "Do not be afraid, for I know that you are looking for Jesus, who was crucified. [6] He is not here; he has risen, just as he said. Come and see the place where he lay. [7] Then go quickly and tell his disciples: 'He has risen from the dead and is going ahead of you into Galilee. There you will see him.' Now I have told you."

Psalms 139:14 I praise you because I am fearfully and wonderfully made; your works are wonderful, I know that full well.

Romans 3:23 for all have sinned and fall short of the glory of God,

Romans 7:14–20 [14] For we know that the law is spiritual, but I am of the flesh, sold under sin. [15] For I do not understand my own actions. For I do not do what I want, but I do the very thing I hate. [16] Now if I do what I do not want, I agree with the law, that it is good. [17] So now it is no longer I who do it, but sin that dwells within me. [18] For I know that nothing good dwells in me, that is, in my flesh. For I have the desire to do what is right, but not the ability to carry it out. [19] For I do not do the good I want, but the evil I do not want is what I keep on doing. [20] Now if I do what I do not want, it is no longer I who do it, but sin that dwells within me.

Romans 8:17 and if children, then heirs—heirs of God and fellow heirs with Christ, provided we suffer with him in order that we may also be glorified with him.

Romans 8:28 And we know that in all things God works for the good of those who love him, who have been called according to his purpose.